Moral Blackmail

Moral Blackmail: Coercion, Responsibility, and Global Justice identifies a novel kind of forced action, yet one that is relatively neglected in ethics and moral philosophy. Moral blackmail occurs when someone is forced to do something because someone else has made all its alternatives morally unacceptable.

Ben Colburn explores moral blackmail by first examining existing theories of coercion, responsibility, and voluntary action, and defending its existence from various sceptical metaethical arguments, before arguing that moral blackmail's significance is not limited to the interpersonal: it is also endemic in the structures of distribution and decision-making at the largest scale. To show this, he considers two problems in intergenerational and international justice: the problem of 'passing the buck' in environmental and population policies in the former, and the problem of 'taking up the slack' in situations of partial compliance with the demands of the latter. Recognising these as instances of moral blackmail writ large offers novel solutions to these long-standing philosophical problems, as well as offering proof in use of the account Colburn proposes.

Moral Blackmail will be of interest to those studying and researching political philosophy, ethical theory, applied ethics, and politics.

Ben Colburn is Professor of Political Philosophy at the University of Glasgow, where he was Head of Philosophy from 2017 to 2020. He is the author of *Autonomy and Liberalism* (2010) and the editor of *The Routledge Handbook of Autonomy* (2022).

Routledge Focus on Philosophy

Routledge Focus on Philosophy is an exciting and innovative new series, capturing and disseminating some of the best and most exciting new research in philosophy in short book form. Peer reviewed and at a maximum of fifty thousand words shorter than the typical research monograph, *Routledge Focus on Philosophy* titles are available in both ebook and print on demand format. Tackling big topics in a digestible format the series opens up important philosophical research for a wider audience, and as such is invaluable reading for the scholar, researcher and student seeking to keep their finger on the pulse of the discipline. The series also reflects the growing interdisciplinarity within philosophy and will be of interest to those in related disciplines across the humanities and social sciences.

Idealism after Existentialism
Encounters in Philosophy of Religion
N.N. Trakakis

State Secrecy and Democracy
A Philosophical Inquiry
Dorota Mokrosinska

The Virtue of Playfulness
Why Happy People are Playful
boomer trujillo

Moral Blackmail
Coercion, Responsibility, and Global Justice
Ben Colburn

For more information about this series, please visit: www.routledge.com/Routledge-Focus-on-Philosophy/book-series/RFP

Moral Blackmail

Coercion, Responsibility, and Global Justice

Ben Colburn

LONDON AND NEW YORK

First published 2025
by Routledge
4 Park Square, Milton Park, Abingdon, Oxon OX14 4RN

and by Routledge
605 Third Avenue, New York, NY 10158

Routledge is an imprint of the Taylor & Francis Group, an informa business

British Library Cataloguing-in-Publication Data
A catalogue record for this book is available from the British Library

Library of Congress Cataloging-in-Publication Data
Names: Colburn, Ben, 1982– author.
Title: Moral Blackmail : coercion, responsibility, and global justice / Ben Colburn.
Description: Abingdon, Oxon ; New York, NY : Routledge, 2025. | Series: Routledge focus on philosophy | Includes bibliographical references and index.
Identifiers: LCCN 2024032878 (print) | LCCN 2024032879 (ebook) | ISBN 9781032195254 (hbk) | ISBN 9781032195292 (pbk) | ISBN 9781003259619 (ebk)
Subjects: LCSH: Choice (Psychology)—Philosophy. | Choice (Psychology)—Social aspects. | Extortion.
Classification: LCC BF611 .C63 2025 (print) | LCC BF611 (ebook) | DDC 153.8/301—dc23/eng/20240814
LC record available at https://lccn.loc.gov/2024032878
LC ebook record available at https://lccn.loc.gov/2024032879

ISBN: 9781032195254 (hbk)
ISBN: 9781032195292 (pbk)
ISBN: 9781003259619 (ebk)

DOI: 10.4324/9781003259619

Typeset in Times New Roman
by codeMantra

To Eric and Liz Colburn, with deep love and thanks.

Contents

Acknowledgements

This book has been a long time in gestation. My thanks to Tony Bruce and Adam Johnson at Routledge for their support and work throughout this project. I have benefited from conversations with many people while developing these ideas. I would like to thank Jessica Begon, Paul Billingham, Michael Brady, Tim Button, Gideon Calder, Amanda Cawston, Jane Clossick, Jennifer Corns, Robert Cowan, Christina Easton, Daniel Elstein, Timothy Endicott, Sarah Fine, Timothy Fowler, Amanda Greene, James Humphries, George Letsas, Hallvard Lillehammer, Brian King, Carl Knight, Stephan Krämer, Matthew Kramer, Katharine Jenkins, Gerald Lang, Finn McCardel, Neil McDonnell, Fiona Macpherson, Paddy McQueen, Chris Mann, Eleanor Mason, Martin O'Neill, Glen Pettigrove, Adam Rieger, Andrew Simester, Joe Slater, Lukas Skiba, Zofia Stemplowska, Christine Straehle, Katy Wells, James Williams, and several anonymous referees. I am also grateful to members of audiences at Birkbeck, Bristol, Cambridge, Edinburgh, Glasgow, Hamburg, Swansea, Tilburg, UCL, Utrecht, Warwick, and on Zoom.

My particular thanks to Jason Park, my catalyst and champion, for many conversations about these ideas over the last twelve years, and also to Serena Olsaretti, for her patient, generous, rigorous support. I began thinking about moral blackmail in postgraduate supervisions between 2003 and 2007, while discussing Serena's important work on freedom, voluntariness, and responsibility. This book is built from concessions I should have made in those arguments twenty years ago; I offer them now, belatedly, with deep gratitude.

Introduction

Suppose I want you to do something. How can I make you do it? Depending on me, you, our context, and the nature of the thing I want you to do, I have various options. Perhaps, if I'm candid about my own motivations, I can rationally or emotionally persuade you to share them. Alternatively, maybe by representing – or even misrepresenting! – things a particular way, I might be able to manipulate you into doing it of your own accord. I might try to force you, perhaps by threatening you if you don't fall in line. This is the familiar phenomenon of coercion, where I tell you that every option except doing what I want will result in unacceptable harm to you. I might even physically compel you to do as I wish. ('Get out of my house!' I shout, as I literally propel you out of the door.)

Depending on the context and the characteristics of the individuals concerned, these different mechanisms will be more or less effective. My ability to rationally persuade you will depend on how cogent my own reasons are, as well as your capacity to grasp them. My ability to physically compel you will depend on my having a significant advantage over you in terms of physical strength. Different mechanisms will also attract different moral evaluations, not settled (or not wholly settled) by their effectiveness. Oftentimes, we might think that deceiving you into doing as I want, or threatening you with violence, is worse than rational persuasion. If I manipulate or coerce you, I'm doing something wrong, perhaps doing *a* wrong to *you*.

This book concerns a mechanism (often effective, usually problematic, and hithertofore generally ignored) whereby individuals can be made to act a certain way, which I call *moral blackmail*. Someone is morally blackmailed into doing something when they are forced to act as they do because all the alternatives are morally unacceptable. Moral blackmail is in this sense analogous to coercion, on a plausible understanding of the latter. It is an interesting and problematic phenomenon in interpersonal dealings. Being able to identify it and distinguish it from other related mechanisms (like compulsion and coercion) is an important addition to our toolkit for understanding our moral psychology and the ethics of our interpersonal dynamics.

DOI: 10.4324/9781003259619-1

The first part of the book develops this basic idea. In Chapter 1, I explain what moral blackmail is, and how it fits into a broader understanding of non-voluntary action. In Chapter 2, I anticipate and respond to likely objections to my proposal, in particular that it makes fundamental mistakes about the force and demandingness of morality. Refuting these objections allows me to clarify the content of what I'm arguing for, and also to head off the reaction that it's implausible.

A further possible objection arises repeatedly when we consider what moral blackmail implies about individual responsibility, in particular that we can in at least one sense be responsible for situations we have not chosen or caused. This worry arises at various points in Chapters 1 and 2. I address it in Chapters 3 and 4 by showing that 'responsibility' is an ambiguous, rather than a univocal, term: the correct theory of responsibility is pluralistic about both the conditions and the consequences of genuine responsibility ascriptions. The phenomenon of moral blackmail, like coercion, works because it prises apart kinds of responsibility that usually sit together. In these two chapters, I set out and motivate that pluralistic theory by explicating, in turn, two central concepts of responsibility. First (in Chapter 3), I explore explanatory responsibility, which obtains when an agent or their decision plays a key role in the explanation of some state of affairs. Then (in Chapter 4), I discuss evaluative responsibility, which obtains when a particular normative upshot for an agent depends on how they in particular relate to a state of affairs. Evaluative responsibility is itself pluralistic, because specific conceptions of evaluative responsibility will be relativised to different potential normative upshots (like praise, blame, reward, compensation, or punishment), and might be grounded by different relations between the agent and the state of affairs in question (including, but not solely, being explanatorily responsible for it). Explaining this theory of responsibility in detail allows us to understand exactly how moral blackmail operates and reveals that the potential objection entertained in Chapters 1 and 2 – that moral blackmail involves us being held responsible inappropriately for situations we don't choose – is based on an equivocation.

Perhaps surprisingly, moral blackmail is not limited to ethically charged interactions between individuals. It is also – indeed, I think, more commonly – a pervasive feature of our societal structures of distribution and decision-making at the largest scale. A central claim of this book is that situations of partial compliance with collective duties (where we all share an obligation to tackle some problem like climate change or global poverty, but where only some of us do our 'fair share') should be understood as instances of moral blackmail writ large. Individuals who do the right thing are effectively morally blackmailed into taking on ever more onerous burdens by those who don't.

The final part of the book extends the account of moral blackmail into this wider political and social context. In Chapters 5 and 6, respectively, I consider two especially difficult problems in intergenerational and international justice: the problem of 'passing the buck' over environmental and population policies in the former, and the problem of 'taking up the slack' in situations of partial compliance with the demands of the latter. Seeing that these are both unacknowledged cases of moral blackmail offers a striking new solution to these problems, by reconciling their two central but apparently contradictory features. In situations of partial compliance, a dutiful agent can have a real complaint against those (either their ancestors or their delinquent contemporaries) who haven't lived up to their duties. In other contexts, complaints of that sort function by default as excuses, showing that the agent should be absolved of the resulting responsibilities. However, in the cases of partial compliance under consideration here, the dutiful agent isn't let off the hook: despite the aptness of their complaint, they nevertheless come to be under heavier duties as a result of other people's non-compliance. How can it be that their moral burdens are made heavier, not lighter, by other people's moral failures?

The resolution offered by a theory of moral blackmail is to say that precisely the force of the dutiful agent's complaint is that they have – blamelessly – come to be subject to those heavier duties. If they *hadn't* come to be genuinely subject to those duties, then they wouldn't have any complaint against their non-complying peers or predecessors. So, the vindication of the complaint is at the same time a confirmation of the moral burden involved. This is a striking result in the political philosophical debates, and also sheds an interesting critical light on the way these matters tend to be discussed in real practical politics too.

1 Moral Blackmail

My first task is to explain what moral blackmail is. That is best done by comparing it with a more commonplace phenomenon, namely coercion, with which it shares many morally relevant features. So, I start by explaining how I understand coercion, and how it fits into a wider account of voluntary and non-voluntary action, before situating moral blackmail in the same account.

1.1 Coercion

Here is a familiar story. You are walking a lonely road at night when you are accosted by a stranger, as threatening as he is debonair. 'Your money or your life!', he declares, pointing a pistol at your head. You don't want to die. So, you comply with his instruction, and hand over your wallet.

This is a paradigm case of coercion. In general, you don't want to give away your money to threatening strangers; you'd not hand it over of your own accord. But the highwayman wants you to, and he makes you do it in this situation. He does so by setting things up so that, when offered the choice (of handing over your money or not), he can rely on you choosing to do what he wants.

How, exactly, does this work?

Some people argue that coercion works – and is presumptively problematic – because it curtails or eliminates free choice. Harry Frankfurt, for example, says that '[a] person who acts under coercion is … regarded as not having acted freely, or of his own free will',[1] and that 'faced with a coercive threat, the victim has no choice but to submit'.[2] J.R. Lucas writes, in a similar vein, that coerced actions are ones which will be 'carried out regardless of the recalcitrance of the [victim]'.[3] Gideon Yaffe says that coercion 'can undermine our freedom' and 'closes or limits options', and that 'freedom is sometimes undermined by [coercion] when it would not be undermined by other causal forces that produce precisely the same actual physical and psychological effects on its victim'.[4]

I think we should reject this freedom-eliminating account of coercion. For one thing, it blurs the difference between two of the central mechanisms

DOI: 10.4324/9781003259619-2

of force that I distinguished at the start of this book, namely coercion and *compulsion.* Imagine, for example, that instead of saying 'Your money or your life!' the highwayman overpowers you with greater physical strength and takes your wallet out of your pocket himself, or wrestles your hands into passing it over. That is compulsion, not coercion. Your freedom of action is eliminated. It is as though you are temporarily an inanimate object which the highwayman puppets as he wishes. There's nothing you can physically do save comply.

Coercion doesn't work like that. The highwayman's threat doesn't eliminate your freedom to make you do what he wants. Rather, he presupposes your free choice and uses it against you, by changing the character of the options you choose between. It remains open to you, in some sense, to reject the option he prefers. You can say 'My life it is, then!', maybe because you think he's overestimated his ability to guarantee your death if you resist, maybe because you prefer resistance-with-death to acquiescence. You *can* do those things but – let us suppose – you don't, because he forces you.[5]

One way of capturing this contrast is to say that compulsion and coercion have different effects on the victim's responsibility for what happens. In cases of compulsion, the victim is in no way responsible. In cases of coercion, the victim's responsibility is eliminated or attenuated in some senses. We generally think they shouldn't be blamed for what happens to them, and perhaps also that they should be compensated for their loss. However, unlike the victim of compulsion, the victim of coercion retains responsibility in the sense that their (coerced) decision to comply is an essential part of the explanation of what happens to them. I will give a more systematic account of this distinction between different senses of responsibility in Chapters 3 and 4, which will vindicate this intuition and make sense of how coercion might undermine responsibility in some ways but not in others. For now, though, I just want to highlight the intuition itself, observing that it gives us a reason to treat coercion differently from compulsion.

To summarise: some accounts of coercion understand it as the elimination of freedom. But these assimilate it to compulsion and fail to accommodate the different effects of this treatment on the victim's responsibility. So, we should reject them for that reason.

Other theorists of coercion hold that it operates not by reducing to one the number of options someone has, and thereby making them unfree, but by changing the nature of those options.[6] That might mean attaching extra burdens to possible actions (after the highwayman makes his threat, every option save handing over your wallet now involves a bullet to the brain), or it might work by making certain conjunctions of outcomes unattainable (even if you retain the disjunctive options of resistance or survival, you no longer have the conjunctive option of resistance *and* survival). This way of thinking about coercion sees it not as an elimination but rather as an exploitation of free choice. The perpetrator forces the victim by setting things up (in particular, by altering the characteristics of the different options they might choose) so that the latter will choose to do as the former wants. They are forced, and their free choice is the *way* that they are forced.[7]

This seems to me a more promising way to understand coercion. It retains the important contrast between coercion and compulsion, and also between coercion and some of the other mechanisms of force surveyed at the start of the book. For example, it makes very clear the difference between manipulation, which depends on the perpetrator deceiving the victim about the number or nature of their options, and coercion, which depends precisely on the perpetrator being honest about those things. It also explains the different effects on responsibility that I mentioned above, and which I explain more fully in Chapters 3 and 4.

1.2 Non-voluntariness

The best way to develop this way of understanding coercion is to see it as a species of what Serena Olsaretti calls 'non-voluntary' action, a category that also encompasses the phenomenon of moral blackmail that is my primary focus in this book. In this section, I expand on what that means.

Olsaretti's account of voluntariness – developed in the context of a critique of Robert Nozick's moralised account of freedom and the libertarian political philosophy that flows from it – is as follows.[8] An act is voluntary if and only if it is not non-voluntary, and non-voluntary if and only if the actor acts as they do because there is no acceptable alternative. This is a criterion with both objective and subjective elements.[9] The standard for acceptability is objective and non-comparative. An alternative is unacceptable if it involves falling below a specified non-comparative level in some measure.[10] For Olsaretti that measure is well-being,[11] but others would do, as long as they don't say that an individual's simply judging an option unacceptable is either necessary or sufficient for settling questions about voluntariness. Nevertheless, the individual's subjective perspective is important, because what matters is whether one acts *because* there are no acceptable alternatives. That is a matter of what one's motivating reasons are, and not (directly) what options one actually has. The condition can be met even if someone as a matter of fact has acceptable alternatives, if they are sincerely mistaken about the number and nature of the options they face, so long as they are nevertheless judging the options they think they have by an appropriate standard of acceptability. For example, the person who is threatened by the highwayman might act non-voluntarily even if as a matter of fact the highwayman was bluffing, and had no ammunition in his pistol, because the victim had good reason to think otherwise, and wasn't applying an inappropriate standard in thinking that being shot would be unacceptable.[12]

Not all cases of non-voluntary action are cases of coercion. Indeed, a key part of Olsaretti's case against Nozick is that one can end up forced into a position of non-voluntary action through the impersonal operation of the free market, including in labour, and that this is problematic even though there need be no intentional coercive action on any other agent's part.[13] Nevertheless, all cases of successful coercion are cases of non-voluntary action. In the story above, the highwayman says, 'Your money or your life!', but he might just as well have said:

> By pointing this loaded gun at you I am altering the character of your options! I hereby make each choice now include a bullet to the head, which I assume to be unacceptable on any objective and non-comparative standard, save only for the option of handing me your money, which I now confidently predict that you will choose!

The paraphrase would lack the picaresque concision of the original threat, but in effect it is exactly the same.

This analysis of coercion as a species of induced non-voluntary action helps us understand how it works. It also helps us explain coercion's moral features, viz. its effects on responsibility and autonomy, and the way it changes the justificatory burdens in situations where it features.

First, coercion undermines responsibility, but only in some senses. As noted above, the victim of coercion retains responsibility in the sense that their decision about what to do (comply or resist?) remains an important part of the explanation of what happens. In other senses, what happens to them does undermine their responsibility. In Olsaretti's terms, borrowed from Thomas Scanlon, their actions remain *attributable* to them, but they lack *substantive responsibility* (so, for example, they shouldn't be blamed, and merit compensation for their loss).[14] Understanding coercion as non-voluntariness explains these different judgements. A non-voluntary decision is still a decision, from the point of view of explaining what happens, but it is a decision for which the individual lacks the kind of responsibility that would make them liable for all of its consequences.[15]

Second, coercion threatens individual autonomy. This is a point of convergence between otherwise quite disparate ways of understanding what autonomy is. For Immanuel Kant, autonomy involved not acting on causes other than what the will provides itself;[16] that includes the strong emotions induced by the actions of others (for example, their coercive threats). Tom Beauchamp and James Childress define autonomy as 'self-rule that is free from … controlling interference by others', where coercion is offered as a paradigm example of such 'controlling interference'.[17] Gerald Dworkin thinks that autonomy consists in having preferences which one endorses under conditions of independence;[18] on this view, coercion introduces disharmony into a person's motivational structure because it arranges things so that their preference for avoiding unacceptable harm conflicts with and dominates all their other endorsed preferences. Joseph Raz, who understands autonomy as an ideal of self-authorship, says that 'autonomy is opposed to a life of coerced choices', because that is not a life that the individual has actively shaped.[19]

I have defended a similar view of autonomy to Raz's, on which autonomy is undermined if someone's responsibility for how their life goes is compromised in either sense.[20] Finally, the most popular contemporary way of understanding autonomy – developed inter alia by Marina Oshana, Natalie Stoljar, and Catriona Mackenzie – sees it as a socio-relational property which is precluded by oppressive relations with others;[21] on this view, coercion either constitutes or is a reliable sign of just such a relation.

I could go on, but the point is clear. Theorists of autonomy converge on the judgement that coercion undermines autonomy. They do so for different reasons, but those reasons can be unified by understanding coercion as a species of non-voluntary action. Some (for example, Kant and Dworkin) concentrate on the distinctive reasons that characterise non-voluntary action; others (for example, Raz and me) focus on the consequences set out above for individual responsibility; yet others (for example, Beauchamp and Childress, Oshana, Stoljar, and Mackenzie) emphasise the malign social relation between the perpetrators and victims of coercion. The common thread is that autonomy is undermined by coercion because coerced action is non-voluntary.

These effects of coercion on responsibility and autonomy explain a third normative feature of coercion, which is that it is often wrong (because of those effects), and in any case always stands in need of justification. Philosophers differ about when and why coercion is justified, but converge on the point that the defender of coercion in a particular action, or domain of action, bears the burden of proof.[22] Understanding coercion as a species of non-voluntary action helps to explain this, and ground it in a wider normative framework.

1.3 From Prudential to Moral Unacceptability

The classic cases of non-voluntariness are prudential. By that, I mean that the standard of acceptability which we use to judge alternatives involves harm to the individual concerned (like a bullet to the brain in the highwayman case). However, there is nothing in the definition of non-voluntary action that means we must understand acceptability this way, so long as the alternatives retain the key features indicated above, namely that an individual's judging an option to be unacceptable is neither necessary nor sufficient for us to deem it actually so, and that it is possible for an individual to be sincerely mistaken about the acceptability of an option while nevertheless deploying an appropriate standard of acceptability.

This feature of the definition of non-voluntariness means that, besides the familiar cases of coercion where unacceptability is grounded in prudential harm, we can have cases that are morally grounded too, where someone acts as they do because all alternatives are *morally*, even if not prudentially, unacceptable. Moreover, it is possible for someone to arrange things that way so as to make someone else act a particular way. Cases of that kind, I suggest, function in many of the same ways as prudential coercion.

Here's an example. Consider the cartoon *Wacky Races*, produced in the late 1960s by Hanna-Barbera for CBS.[23] The premise of the series is that eleven cars are racing for the title 'World's Wackiest Racer', using entertaining means to try to win each episode's race. The villains of the piece are the characters Dastardly and Muttley, whose main tactic is to use underhand (and not merely wacky) means to win, seeking to stymie their competitors and cheat their way to victory.

Suppose that in one episode Dastardly and Muttley are inspired by reading some famous normative ethical thought experiments[24] and hatch the following scheme to beat you (as one of their competitors; you can choose whether to be Penelope Pitstop, Rufus Ruffcat, or one of the others). Getting ahead of the field, they throw a baby into a shallow and secluded pond, before zooming off. Soon afterwards, you arrive at that part of the track, you see what has happened. You can save the baby – it's a very shallow pond, and you'd not be at any personal risk – and there's nobody else around who can. So, you should save the baby, and you do, and in so doing fall far enough behind Dastardly and Muttley that you lose the race.

This is a literally and deliberately cartoonish example. It might give the mistaken impression that the phenomenon I am interested in is something existing only in dramatic vignettes like children's stories or philosophers' thought experiments, and therefore too peripheral and stylised to be useful. As it happens, I think dramatic vignettes are sometimes a defensible way to explore our ethical concepts, in part precisely *because* they are stylised, simplified, and selective.[25] In any case, though, this phenomenon is not limited to those contexts. I turn to less cartoonish instances in Chapters 5 and 6, where I show that it is a prominent and troubling feature of our real-world ethical interactions, specifically situations of partial compliance with onerous collective duties. I think the material there should reassure the reader who currently doubts whether reflection on Wacky Races is a sensible use of their time.

Nevertheless, the present artificial example is useful because it makes very clear the parallels between this case and the highwayman case discussed above. In both cases, the wrongdoer makes you act a particular way not by constraining your freedom, but rather by altering the character of your options. Admittedly, they do that in different ways. The highwayman does it by threatening prudential harm to you if you don't hand over your money, whereas Dastardly and Muttley do it by appending a weighty moral cost to your non-compliance. But the structure, and the basic explanation for your action, is the same in both cases: you have exercised your free choice to select one option for the reason that all its alternatives are in some way unacceptable.

So, if we recognise coercion as a (generally) problematic phenomenon, and accept that it is a species of non-voluntary action on Olsaretti's account, we should say the same things about a case of the latter kind, which differs only in that it is moral and not prudential considerations that make the alternatives unacceptable. Like more straightforward coercion, this kind of treatment undermines the recipient's responsibility in some senses (but not all); it always undermines autonomy; and it is often wrong, and so always stands in need of justification, even if there can be innocuous instances.

I propose to call this kind of case 'moral blackmail'. That is not the only possible name for it. We might, for example, call it 'moral coercion', to emphasise the parallel with (prudential) coercion of the sort we see in the highwayman case.[26] This terminological choice would head off the worry that the kind of situation I describe lacks some of the characteristic features of blackmail as it is usually defined in the law, such as the demand's being 'unwarranted'.[27] Nevertheless, and with due deference to legal usage and analysis of the term 'blackmail',[28] 'moral blackmail' is the term I use. It has a distinct and non-legally defined meaning in everyday ethical talk; it is familiar and apt for the phenomenon I'm describing. My using it also aligns with some of the few others in the literature who have explored phenomena in this domain. For example, Terrence McConnell uses the term to refer to situations where 'we are in a unique position to prevent someone from doing a greater evil, but only by doing a lesser evil ourselves [and] have been placed in this unique position by someone else'.[29] More recently, Simon Keller considers 'a wrongful act that forces someone to do something by making her alternatives morally unacceptable', and calls this kind of act 'moral blackmail'.[30] McConnell and Keller both have in mind narrower phenomena than I am examining here, as will become especially clear when I move to considering moral blackmail in political philosophy in Chapters 5 and 6. But the basic concept – of someone being forced to do something because the alternatives are all morally unacceptable – is the same.

To conclude: there exists a phenomenon of moral blackmail. It is a close relative of coercion. Like coercion, it involves an agent being made to act a particular way not through the elimination of their free choice, but through its exploitation: things are arranged so that all alternatives to the target action are unacceptable, with the result that the agent takes that action non-voluntarily. In classic coercion, the grounds of unacceptability are prudential, usually a threat of severe harm to the victim. In moral blackmail, the perpetrator weaponises morality against the victim, by making the alternatives morally unacceptable. This contrast notwithstanding, the moral effects are the same: the victim's responsibility and autonomy are undermined, and so moral blackmail is often wrong, and always stands in need of justification.

Notes

1 H. Frankfurt 'Coercion and Moral Responsibility' in his *The Importance of What We Care About: Philosophical Essays*, Cambridge: Cambridge University Press, 1988: pp. 26–46, at 26–27.

2 H. Frankfurt 'Coercion and Moral Responsibility' in his *The Importance of What We Care About: Philosophical Essays*, Cambridge: Cambridge University Press, 1988: pp. 26–46, at 40.

3 E.g. J.R. Lucas *The Principles of Politics*, Oxford: Clarendon Press, 1966: p. 57.

4 G. Yaffe 'Indoctrination, Coercion, and Freedom of Will', *Philosophy and Phenomenological Research* 67 (2003): 335–356, at 335.

5 The highwayman's threat might amount to compulsion for some victims, if e.g. the prospect of death is so disturbing that the latter is *psychologically* incapable of resisting. It is the impossibility of doing otherwise, not *physical* impossibility alone, that is the mark of compulsion, and fear can make actions impossible, as those who suffer from extreme phobias know. Nevertheless, coercion doesn't *depend* on such a psychological reaction for its power or its presumptive wrongness.

6 E.g., R. Nozick 'Coercion', in P. Lazlett & W. Runciman eds. *Philosophy, Politics, and Society* (4th series), Oxford: Blackwell, 1967: pp. 101–135; B. Gert 'Coercion and Freedom', in J.R. Pennock & J.W. Chapman eds. *Coercion*, Piscataway, NJ: Transaction Publishers, 1972: pp. 30–48; D. Zimmerman 'Coercive Wage Offers', *Philosophy & Public Affairs* 20 (1981): 121–125; J. Feinberg *Harm to Self*, New York: Oxford University Press, 1986: pp. 192–194; A. Wertheimer *Coercion*, Princeton, NJ: Princeton University Press, 1988: pp. 5–6; C. Carr 'Coercion and Freedom', *American Philosophical Quarterly* 25 (1988): 59–67; S. Olsaretti *Liberty, Desert and the Market*, Cambridge: Cambridge University Press, 2004: pp. 141–148; and E. Mason 'Coercion and Integrity', in M. Timmons ed. *Oxford Studies in Normative Ethics: Volume 2*, Oxford: Oxford University Press, 2012: pp. 180–205.

7 Indeed, in some circumstances, someone might be forced by their freedom being increased, that is by a new *offer* which leaves their existing options untouched. These circumstances are rare, for reasons I explain in note 10.

8 Originally 'Freedom, Force and Choice: Against the Rights-Based Definition of Voluntariness', *Journal of Political Philosophy* 6 (1998): 53–78 and 'The Value of Freedom and Freedom of Choice', *Politeia* 56 (2000): 114–121, but the locus classicus is her *Liberty, Desert and the Market*, Cambridge: Cambridge University Press, 2004: pp. 141–148.

9 I originally discussed this in 'The Concept of Voluntariness', *Journal of Political Philosophy* 16 (2008): 101–111.

10 The requirement that unacceptability is judged non-comparatively pre-empts the worry that some actions – plausibly, most actions! – might otherwise count as non-voluntary just because, if the option picked is the best in an agent's choice set, the other options are in a sense rationally unacceptable. This comparative test for unacceptability is irrelevant for judgements about voluntariness, at least in the sense that's morally and politically relevant. This, incidentally, is also what explains why it is rare that someone might be coerced by giving them an *offer* while leaving their other options unchanged. Such an offer might be so good that the other options come to be comparatively unacceptable, but if they weren't non-comparatively unacceptable before the offer, then they're not so afterwards, and the individual doesn't act non-voluntarily in choosing the new offer. This echoes Hillel Steiner's way of distinguishing offers from threats: the costs of non-compliance with the former are comparative, and with the latter absolute. ('Individual Liberty', *Proceedings of the Aristotelian Society* 75 (1974): 33–50, at 38–39.) My thanks to an anonymous referee for noting the parallel.

11 S. Olsaretti *Liberty, Desert and the Market*, Cambridge: Cambridge University Press, 2004: p. 139.

12 B. Colburn 'The Concept of Voluntariness', *Journal of Political Philosophy* 16 (2008): 101–111, where I argue that this subjective aspect of voluntariness cuts both ways: someone might act voluntarily despite the absence of any acceptable alternatives because they falsely believe that that is not the case. See also S. Olsaretti 'The Concept of Voluntariness – A Reply', *Journal of Political Philosophy* 16 (2008): 112–121.

13 S. Olsaretti *Liberty, Desert and the Market*, Cambridge: Cambridge University Press, 2004: p. 150.
14 S. Olsaretti *Liberty, Desert and the Market*, Cambridge: Cambridge University Press, 2004: pp. 158–159, and see T.M. Scanlon 'The Significance of Choice' in S. McMullin ed. *The Tanner Lectures on Human Values*, Vol. 8, Salt Lake City: University of Utah Press, 1988: pp. 149–216, reprinted in *What We Owe to Each Other*, Cambridge, MA: Harvard University Press, 1998: Chapter 6.
15 S. Olsaretti *Liberty, Desert and the Market*, Cambridge: Cambridge University Press, 2004: p. 161.
16 I. Kant *Grundlegung zur Metaphysik der Sitten*, originally published 1785. Ed. & trans. by M. Gregor as *Groundwork of the Metaphysics of Morals*, Cambridge: Cambridge University Press, 1994: §3.
17 E.g. T. Beauchamp & J.F. Childress *Principles of Biomedical Ethics* (5th edition), New York: Oxford University Press, 2001: p. 58.
18 G. Dworkin *The Theory and Practice of Autonomy*, Cambridge: Cambridge University Press, 1988. See also H. Frankfurt 'Freedom of the Will and the Concept of a Person', *Journal of Philosophy* 68 (1971): 5–20.
19 J. Raz *The Morality of Freedom*, Oxford: Clarendon Press, 1986: pp. 369, 371.
20 B. Colburn *Autonomy and Liberalism*, New York: Routledge, 2010. I say more about this view of autonomy in Chapter 6.
21 M. Oshana *Personal Autonomy in Society*, Aldershot: Ashgate, 2006; C. Mackenzie & N. Stoljar eds. *Relational Autonomy: Feminist Perspectives on Autonomy, Agency, and the Social* Self, New York: Oxford University Press, 2000.
22 E.g. C.C. Ryan 'The Normative Concept of Coercion', *Mind* 89 (1980): 481–498; J. Rawls *Political Liberalism*, New York: Columbia University Press, 1993: p. 58; E. Mason 'Coercion and Integrity', in M. Timmons ed. *Oxford Studies in Normative Ethics: Volume 2*, Oxford: Oxford University Press, 2012; S. White 'On the Moral Objection to Coercion', *Philosophy & Public Affairs* 45 (2017): 199–231; M. Garnett 'Coercion: The Wrong and the Bad', *Ethics* 128 (2018): 545–573.
23 *Wacky Races*. Hanna-Barbera Productions, for CBS. WBBM-TV, Chicago, 1968–1969.
24 Specifically, P. Singer 'Famine, Affluence and Morality', *Philosophy & Public Affairs* 1 (1972): 229–243, at 231.
25 B. Colburn 'Dramatic Vignettes in Moral Inquiry', *Social Analysis* 68 (2024): 66–74.
26 This is the term used by Saba Bazargan to explore a similar phenomenon, albeit that Bazargan doesn't understand coercion in terms of non-voluntariness as I do. ('Moral Coercion', *Philosophers' Imprint* 14 (2014): 3–5.) Other options include 'moral constraint' or 'moral containment'; I'm grateful to Jennifer Corns for those attempts to find *le mot juste*.
27 *Theft Act* 1968 (UK). https://www.legislation.gov.uk/ukpga/1968/60/pdfs/ukpga_19680060_en.pdf [accessed 11 March 2024: §21]. There are similar conditions in other legal codes.
28 See e.g. the useful survey and critical discussion in M. Berman 'Blackmail', in J. Deigh & D. Dolinko eds. *The Oxford Handbook of Criminal Law*, Oxford: Oxford University Press, 2011: pp. 37–105. My thanks to an anonymous referee for making it clear that it would be useful to emphasise the distinctness of my concept of *moral blackmail* from the legal concept of 'blackmail'.
29 T. McConnell 'Moral Blackmail', *Ethics* 91 (1981): 544–567, 545.
30 S. Keller 'Fiduciary Duties and Moral Blackmail', *The Journal of Applied Philosophy* 35 (2018): 481–495.

2 The Force of Morality

Chapter 1 introduced the idea of moral blackmail, a phenomenon wherein an agent can be forced to act in a particular way because someone has made all the alternatives morally unacceptable. Acting from moral blackmail is a type of non-voluntary action, analogous to the more familiar phenomenon of prudential coercion, wherein someone is forced to act a certain way because someone has made all the alternatives *prudentially* unacceptable.

A key element of this analysis is that it treats both kinds of unacceptability in the same way, at least for the purpose of judging whether someone acts voluntarily or not. This is not to deny that, depending on one's background ethical theory, there might be a big difference between something's being prudentially unacceptable and its being morally unacceptable. We might think the (impersonal) normative weightiness of these considerations are very different, and that the psychological accounts of what it is to be motivated by them will also diverge. It seems plausible, for example, that acting to avoid prudential unacceptability – as when someone is threatened with violence – will usually involve intense emotions like fear, whereas an intense emotional state isn't typically associated with moral action, at least if it's decoupled from those sorts of dramatic prudential threats. The view set out in Chapter 1 doesn't seek to ignore or downplay those contrasts between considerations of prudence and morality. Neither, indeed, does it presuppose that they are sharply distinct. The person who thinks that moral unacceptability must ultimately be grounded in prudential concerns,[1] and the person who thinks that doing morally unacceptable things is (inter alia) prudentially bad for us,[2] can both accept that moral blackmail is a real phenomenon. The central point is that it is the unacceptability *as such* of alternatives that renders action non-voluntary, and that moral factors can ground unacceptability just as well as the prospect of prudential harm.

Nevertheless, at this point, someone might raise a different sort of worry about the account I have given here, which turns not on what it says about the relationship between morality and prudence, but rather on what it assumes about the nature of morality itself. Specifically, the worry might arise that it misunderstands the *force* of morality to think that there is a meaningful and

DOI: 10.4324/9781003259619-3

interesting class of actions we might label 'moral blackmail' as defined in Chapter 1. I have in mind here two lines of argument. The first is the worry that my account of moral blackmail depends on the implausible claim that morality *forces* us to do as it requires. Moral force just doesn't work like that, so the argument goes. So, no action is ever morally blackmailed. The second is the worry that every moral choice is forced in this way, because it's always unacceptable to pick any action which isn't the one morality requires. So, every action – or at least every *moral* action – is morally blackmailed.

Either conclusion would be a problem for me, since each implies that moral blackmail is not a distinct and problematic phenomenon, either because it's non-existent or because it's endemic. So, in this chapter, I consider and respond to these two criticisms, arguing that they don't give reason to reject the analysis of moral blackmail I gave in Chapter 1.

2.1 Impossibility

Shelley Kagan, writing about the demandingness of morality, writes that:

> … morality itself cannot violate a constraint by requiring that agents make some sacrifice—for morality cannot literally coerce the agent or *force* her to make the sacrifice. A moral requirement exists when there is a morally decisive reason for an agent to react in a given way. But the mere *existence* of such a reason hardly forces the individual to react appropriately. Thus moral requirement is quite unlike external interference or coercion; and, for that matter, it is also quite unlike internal (physical or psychological) disability, or other limiting or disabling factors (such as the lack of resources). The existence of a moral requirement per se simply does not limit our abilities.[3]

Kagan's is an unusually explicit statement, so I treat it as my stalking horse for this section, but I think it captures a widespread view.[4] That view is something like this: when we speak of moral 'force' we are speaking metaphorically; construing it literally, as though moral force is the same thing as physical or psychological force, with the same effects, is simply confused.

The worry for present purposes is that, once we realise this, the plausibility of my account of moral blackmail dissolves, because it turns out to be based on a pun. The apparent instrument of 'force' in the case of moral blackmail (viz. the moral unacceptability of someone's alternatives) cannot operate the same way as the threat of prudential harm in coercion, because in reality it's no kind of force at all.

As my remarks in Chapter 1 should make clear, I think Kagan is right that morality, prudence, and compulsion work differently. Indeed, part of the interest of moral blackmail as a topic of inquiry depends on that very fact, specifically on the distinctive effects it has on individual responsibility. (I alluded to those briefly in Chapter 1 and return to them at the end of Chapter 4.) Nevertheless, I think we should reject the next step in Kagan's reasoning, namely that these dissimilarities disbar morality from having the kind of force that can sometimes make for something like coercion. The passage quoted above suggests two different ways we might understand that step of Kagan's, but isn't clear about which one is doing the real work. In this section, I argue that the plausibility of this attack on moral blackmail depends on those different lines of thought being conflated. Once they're disentangled and examined separately, I don't think that either is persuasive in ruling out moral blackmail as a real phenomenon.

First, Kagan comments that 'the mere *existence* of [a moral requirement] hardly forces the individual to react appropriately' (his emphasis).[5] That is true, and it evokes the august question of how morality is binding when it is neither physically nor psychologically necessitating.[6] Thankfully, for present purposes we don't need to answer that question. The question for us is whether Kagan's point undermines my account of moral blackmail, by drawing a line between moral requirement on the one hand and (prudential) coercion on the other.

The answer is that it doesn't, for reasons given in the previous chapter: it is true of coercion, too, that 'the mere *existence*' of a prudential requirement doesn't force the actor in the sense Kagan means either. For one thing, as I noted above, whether an action is non-voluntary depends on what the agent's motivating reasons are, and hence what their beliefs are about their options, rather than – directly – on the existence and nature of those options themselves. Possessing only unacceptable alternatives is neither sufficient nor necessary for coercion to take place.[7] For another thing, even if we stipulate that an individual has true beliefs about their options – and in fairness that will usually be the case with coercion, since the perpetrator's technique works by making their victim aware of their predicament[8] – they retain their freedom to choose in cases of coercion. The highwayman's victim *can* say 'My life, then!' As I said above, coercion exploits, rather than eliminates, free choice. In this sense, it is unlike compulsion.

So, this first version of Kagan's argument doesn't rule out moral blackmail. For that to happen, he would have to draw a sharp line between force (which for Kagan means physical compulsion, I think) and coercion on the one hand, and moral requirement on the other. In fact, the line he describes sits between compulsion and the other two phenomena. So (prudential) coercion and moral blackmail stand or fall together on Kagan's reasoning. Since we should plainly not on these grounds reject the former as a way we can be made to act, the latter likewise emerges unscathed.

Kagan's second thought contrasts moral requirement not with coercion (and compulsion), but with factors like internal disabilities or external limitations. Unlike those things, he says, '[the] existence of a moral requirement per se simply does not limit our abilities'.[9] That seems true enough. When we act as we do because of a moral requirement, that is because we have exercised our abilities of moral discernment and agency, not because our abilities have been limited.

As before, though, I don't think this eliminates moral blackmail, for three reasons. First, there is something question-begging about the move. If the claim under examination is that moral blackmail is a distinct way that we can be made to act that doesn't depend on 'limiting our abilities', then merely asserting that it is in this respect dissimilar to (for example) physical force, psychological disability, or external limitation doesn't get us very far: it is a mere restatement of the claim to be proved. Second, everything I have said so far about Kagan's previous argument applies again to this one. Coercion too doesn't 'limit our abilities', and instead works precisely by exploiting those abilities (specifically, our capacity for self-interested rationality to avoid anticipated harm).[10] So, the same problem arises as before. We should deny the existence of moral blackmail on Kagan's grounds only if we are prepared to deny the existence of prudential coercion. That is implausible. So, we should not deny the existence of moral blackmail.

Maybe the problem that Kagan envisages is not process but modal effect: the point is not that 'limiting our abilities' is intrinsically a problematic mechanism, but rather that it – unlike 'moral requirement' – makes it in some sense impossible to act otherwise, rather than merely impermissible. Setting aside the worry that this still doesn't distinguish moral blackmail from prudential coercion, the shift to the modal criterion raises a third worry, which is especially weighty if we think about the political implications of these arguments. On this reading, the 'proper' cases on Kagan's list count because the restriction of our abilities makes actions (other than the one we're pushed into) impossible. In reality, cases like this are rare. No doubt, there will be some actions which physical or psychological disability, or lack of external resources, make literally impossible for us. But there will be many more actions for which those things merely raise the costs dramatically. Severe mobility restrictions don't necessarily make it impossible to (for example) complete a marathon; they just make it very hard. Lack of external resources likewise doesn't make all resource-expensive action impossible; it just increases the opportunity costs of devoting one's limited resources to *this* action, constraining one's ability to achieve various outcomes at the same time. If strict impossibility (rather than just painfully increased costs) is what matters, then most of the familiar instances of force which Kagan alludes to will be ruled out alongside moral requirement (and prudential coercion). At the very least, that generates another companions-in-guilt defence for moral blackmail. But I think that the political philosophical implications here – for example, that the limitations involved in disability and poverty aren't really problematic unless they involve strict impossibility – are sufficiently unpalatable that they constitute a reductio ad absurdum of this way of trying to defend Kagan's line.

My focus here has been narrowly on Kagan, but the points I have made apply more generally. One might feel some intuitive resistance to the idea that moral unacceptability can have the kind of 'force' required to generate a coercion-like phenomenon of moral blackmail. Even if that resistance is grounded in genuine insight (for example, about the ways in which morality is and is not binding), it is not a good reason to reject the claim that moral blackmail exists as a species of induced non-voluntary action, at least if one isn't willing for the same reason to reject all coercion, and some other plausible instances of force besides. So, I think it is safe to conclude that morality can at least sometimes have the kind of force required for moral blackmail to be a real phenomenon.

2.2 Ubiquity

At this point, another worry might arise. This is not, as in the previous section, that moral blackmail as I define it cannot happen, but rather that my definition implies that it is endemic, because the considerations I gave in Section 2.1 prove too much: they imply that all morally required action is non-voluntary.

Here is the argument. Suppose that I am facing a choice about how to act. I see that one of the options I have is morally required, and I act accordingly. It seems as though when I do so, I act because no other action is acceptable. That was just what it *means* to say that the option I picked was morally required. But in that case, it looks as though whenever I act morally (meaning that I do the right thing because morality demands it), I act non-voluntarily. Depending on how far we think morality gives us a determinate single answer whenever we have a choice about how to act, this might mean that a large proportion of our choices are non-voluntary in Olsaretti's sense: everything that isn't immoral, capricious, or the subject of a strict moral dilemma, in fact.[11]

This objection might be advanced with two different dialectical payoffs in mind. One way of understanding it treats the conclusion – that almost all moral acts are non-voluntary – as false, indeed absurd. It therefore takes the argument as a reductio ad absurdum, and a disproof of the key premise, that moral unacceptability can make for non-voluntariness. That might be because the conclusion strikes the reader as manifestly indefensible, or maybe (more likely) because it has some further implications of that kind. One might object, for example, that if all moral acts are non-voluntary, then one is never responsible for acting voluntarily, and hence that one never merits praise for doing the right thing. In either case, the idea is that we should reject the idea of moral blackmail because of the absurdity of these implications.[12]

The other way of understanding the objection accepts that conclusion (that almost all moral acts are non-voluntary) as true. So, it concludes that since almost no action is voluntary in Olsaretti's sense, voluntariness cannot be (as she and I both argue) the grounds of differential judgements of, for example, responsibility or autonomy.

Either way of construing the objection is a problem for my position. The first implies that moral blackmail doesn't really exist. The second implies that if it exists, it doesn't pick out anything problematic, and has none of the problematic consequences I identified in Chapter 1 (and explore further in Chapters 5 and 6).

The key claim underpinning the objection – whether construed as a reductio ad absurdum or as an attack on the distinct moral significance of non-voluntariness – is that the alternatives to a morally required action are *ipso facto* unacceptable. One might reject that, as for example Dan Brock does when (in the context of a debate about the demandingness of morality) he argues that a correct moral theory must always preserve 'moral options' for action.[13] But even if we concede the point, there are two ways to resist this argument against moral blackmail and its significance. First, it doesn't follow from the fact that it is unacceptable to do other than what morality demands that all morally required action is non-voluntary. Second, even if we thought that did follow, there would still be a reason to think that cases of moral blackmail are especially problematic, and hence can be distinguished, for practical purposes, from the much wider class of morally required actions.

To expand on the first point: in Chapter 1, I explained that the voluntariness of an action depends primarily on the agent's motivating reasons, and therefore only indirectly on the real qualities of the options they face, to the extent that those qualities feature in their motivating reasons. It is possible for someone to be in a situation where, as a matter of fact, they have no acceptable alternatives to a course of action, but where they nevertheless act voluntarily because the absence of acceptable alternatives isn't their motivating reason. That might be because they falsely believe that the alternatives were acceptable.[14] Alternatively, and more relevantly for us, they might be motivated by the intrinsic qualities of the option they pick, rather than its contrast with the alternatives, as in Olsaretti's case of the Wired City:

> Wendy is the inhabitant of a city fenced with electrifying wire, which she is unfree to leave. However, her city has all that anyone could ever ask for, and Wendy, who is perfectly happy with her life there, has no wish of leaving it. She voluntarily remains in her city.[15]

Without wanting to venture a general account of moral motivation, I suggest that it often has a structure similar to Wendy's motivation as Olsaretti describes it. While the alternatives are unacceptable (prudentially in Wendy's case, morally in ours), that is not the feature of the cases that explains our actions. In Wendy's case her motivating reason is the excellence of the city itself, not the presence of the electrifying wire. In the case of much moral action, the motivating reason is just the rightness of the option pursued.[16] It might be a necessary consequence of that rightness that the alternatives are unacceptable – in this respect, the cases are perhaps disanalogous – but that consequence need not be part of the agent's motivation, and its mere ubiquity is no reason to think that, in most cases, it will be. The main cases where it *will* be are cases where an agent is antecedently motivated to pick some other option which then comes to be unacceptable, with the result that they reject it for an alternative they previously didn't favour. But these are exactly the cases of which moral blackmail is the paradigm, so their turning out to be non-voluntary is not a problem for me. In fact it is exactly the result that we should expect if my account is correct.

Let me turn to my second response. When we talk about moral blackmail, we are considering a special kind of situation, where the explanation for the alternatives being morally unacceptable is that someone else has made them so (either deliberately or inadvertently). So, even if my opponent is unpersuaded by the argument above, and maintains that much moral action is non-voluntary because moral motivation *is* in general about avoiding morally unacceptable alternatives, I can still sustain what is most important in my view, namely that moral blackmail is a distinctive and problematic phenomenon. That is because moral blackmail is unusual insofar as it involves non-voluntariness *imposed by others*. The protagonist of Wacky Races must save the baby not just because morality demands it, but also because Dastardly and Muttley contrived to put them that morally charged situation. The point is analogous to one made by some theorists of freedom: even if any external impediment might make someone unable to do what they want, it is only external impediments *imposed by other people* that make them unfree, in a sense that will be problematic for a liberty-minded political theory.[17]

So, even if the reader thinks moral action is ipso facto non-voluntary, and that undermines the idea that non-voluntariness is problematic as such, I can still maintain that moral blackmail is distinctive and problematic because it is non-voluntariness imposed by others. For now, I leave open exactly how to understand the idea of 'imposition' here. In the cartoon case, it is intentionally caused by our antagonists: Dastardly and Muttley deliberately manufacture a scenario to force our protagonist, in particular, to lose the race. We might think that this intentional targeting of a specific victim is the paradigm case of moral blackmail. I don't think it is the only type of case which has these structural features, though. In Chapters 5 and 6, I go on to consider cases with no identifiable intention to morally blackmail, no individual agent doing the moral blackmailing, and where there was no specific victim targeted at all, albeit that – if I am right – there are victims. Even then, the structural effect of the (perhaps unwitting) perpetrators on the decision-making of the victim has all the problematic features I have picked out.

To conclude: I have considered and addressed two objections to my proposal that moral blackmail is a real and significant phenomenon. I have shown that one shouldn't reject this proposal on the grounds that moral unacceptability never has the kind of force that can lead to non-voluntary action. I have also shown that one shouldn't reject it on the grounds that the conclusion overgeneralises and hence collapses into absurdity, or implies that moral blackmail is no more problematic than instances of moral blackmail in general. In the course of responding to such worries, I have refined the way we should understand moral blackmail, in particular by specifying that it must involve non-voluntariness imposed by other agents in some way. That might mean the kind of intentional and specific victimisation present in the cartoon example in Chapter 1 which I have relied on so far. But those features aren't essential. In Chapters 5 and 6, I discuss important cases of moral blackmail that don't involve specific intent by the perpetrator, but where the perpetrator's actions (which are, in general, to avoid moral burdens which they should otherwise bear) nevertheless have the same problematic effect on their victims.

Before I move on to those cases, I consider a further line of resistance. At various points, both in setting out my position in Chapter 1 and in defending it in this chapter, I have relied on distinguishing between different senses of responsibility, for example, by saying that what marks out prudential coercion and moral blackmail from physical compulsion is that the former, unlike the latter, target the victim's responsibility in only some senses, while leaving others intact. This way of understanding responsibility, on which the term is not treated as univocal, needs to be justified for my view of moral blackmail to work, and it also merits exploration on its own terms. I turn to that task in the next two chapters.

Notes

1 This is true of classic utilitarians like Bentham in *An Introduction to the Principles of Morals and Legislation*, originally published 1789, ed. J.H. Burns & H.L.A Hart, London: Athlone Press, 1970. A more recent example is M. Arvan *Neurofunctional Prudence and Morality: A Philosophical Theory*, New York: Routledge, 2020: pp. 60–89.

2 E.g. Plato 'Gorgias' in M. Schofield ed. & T. Griffin trans. *Plato: Gorgias, Menexenus, Protagoras*, Cambridge: Cambridge University Press, 2009: pp. 1–114. Under some interpretations Ronald Dworkin was a modern proponent of a more restricted version of this thesis, insofar as he believed that someone's doing *unjust* things couldn't contribute to their life going well. See R. Dworkin *Sovereign Virtue*, Cambridge, MA: Harvard University Press, 2000: pp. 237–284.

3 S. Kagan *The Limits of Morality*, Oxford: Clarendon Press 1989: p. 238.

4 Others have made similar points, including me in B. Colburn 'The Concept of Voluntariness', *Journal of Political Philosophy* 16 (2008): pp. 104–106. There, I argued (against an objection in correspondence from Olsaretti) that only prudential unacceptability counts for non-voluntariness, because moral unacceptability lacks 'a similar instrument of force' to the prudential case. (The present book recants that argument.)

5 S. Kagan *The Limits of Morality*, Oxford: Clarendon Press 1989: p. 238.

6 This is not to deny that demands of morality might be experienced as psychologically necessitating by some. Martin Luther is famously quoted as saying 'Here I stand, I can do no other' when pressed at the 1521 Diet of Worms to recant his 95 Theses. Harry Frankfurt and Bernard Williams discuss these cases as instances of a kind of 'volitional necessity', to use Frankfurt's term. See H. Frankfurt 'The

Importance of What We Care About' in his *The Importance of What We Care About*, Cambridge: Cambridge University Press, 1988: pp. 80–94, at p. 87; B. Williams 'Moral Incapacity' in his *Making Sense of Humanity*, Cambridge: Cambridge University Press, 1995: pp. 46–55. Nevertheless, experiencing the demands of morality in this way isn't required for moral action. Indeed we might think there's something dysfunctional (and not morally admirable) about the agent who assimilates moral to psychological necessity in this way. Susan Wolf thinks that understanding moral action this way would preclude the praise that someone deserves when they do the right thing for the right reason ('Asymmetrical Freedom', *Journal of Philosophy* 77 (1980): 151–166, at 156–157). Michael Smith calls such a person a 'moral fetishist' (*The Moral Problem*, Oxford: Blackwell, 1994: p. 76). To put it provocatively, the person who understands Luther as saying 'Here I stand, I am psychologically incapable of doing otherwise' doesn't really understand what moral force *is*.

7 B. Colburn 'The Concept of Voluntariness', *Journal of Political Philosophy* 16 (2008): pp. 102–103.

8 This is not so for threats that are bluffs, of course, but those will still be cases of non-voluntary action, since what matters for voluntariness is the actor's beliefs about what their options are, not what they *actually* are. My thanks to Matthew Kramer for raising this question.

9 S. Kagan *The Limits of Morality*, Oxford: Clarendon Press 1989: p. 238.

10 This is not to say that there aren't other contrasts between prudential coercion and moral blackmail, e.g., that in the latter someone's abilities are (by definition) always redirected at a morally permissible (indeed, required) end, whereas in the former they are directed to the fulfilment of the coercer's wishes. The point is just that there is no contrast between the two categories specifically on the question of whether one's abilities are *limited*, as Kagan suggested. My thanks to Gerald Lang for pressing this point.

11 This is an argument I first developed in B. Colburn 'The Concept of Voluntariness', *Journal of Political Philosophy* 16 (2008): pp. 103–105.

12 Not everyone would regard these implications as absurd. Someone might simply accept that we don't merit praise for doing what is morally required, for example. Alternatively, they might distinguish between different senses of responsibility to say that, even if we aren't responsible for our moral actions in some sense, we remain so in others, and hence avoid the unpalatable implication by saying that we remain praiseworthy. That is Olsaretti's reply (in S. Olsaretti 'The Concept of Voluntariness – A Reply', *Journal of Political Philosophy* 16 (2008): 112–121) to the argument in B. Colburn 'The Concept of Voluntariness', *Journal of Political Philosophy* 16 (2008): 101–111. Whether or not someone finds that reply reassuring will depend on the attitude they take to the pluralistic view of responsibility I develop in Chapters 3 and 4. Still, one might be unmoved by those attempts to remove or mitigate the apparent absurdity of the conclusion, so it is worth taking the objection seriously, and scrutinising (as I do below) the reasoning that leads to its conclusion.

13 D. Brock 'Defending Moral Options', *Philosophy & Phenomenological Research* 51 (1991): 909–931, at 912.

14 E.g. B. Colburn 'The Concept of Voluntariness', *Journal of Political Philosophy* 16 (2008): 102–103.

15 S. Olsaretti *Liberty, Desert and the Market*, Cambridge: Cambridge University Press, 2004: p. 138. I discuss a similar case in B. Colburn *Autonomy and Liberalism*, New York: Routledge, 2010 at p. 99.

16 This might mean that the acceptability of the option picked features in the agent's motivation, but it doesn't entail that the unacceptability of other options does. My thanks to an anonymous referee for pressing this point.

17 E.g. H. Steiner *An Essay on Rights*, Oxford: Blackwell, 1994: pp. 6–54; M.H. Kramer *The Quality of Freedom*, Oxford: Oxford University Press, 2003: p. 3.

3 Explanatory Responsibility

The arguments in Chapters 1 and 2 turn, in part, on distinguishing between different kinds of responsibility. In Chapter 1, I argued that we should consider coercion different from compulsion at least in part because these two mechanisms – albeit that they both involve one agent making another do what they want – have different effects on the recipient's responsibility: compulsion undermines responsibility in all senses, whereas coercion undermines it only in some. Specifically, coercion removes or reduces the extent to which the victim is responsible in the senses relevant to ascriptions of praise or blame, or punishment, reward, and compensation, but it leaves intact the role that the recipient's decision played in determining the outcome. Moral blackmail, I suggested, has some of the same effects on responsibility. We can draw on similar considerations to further defang some of the arguments against moral blackmail I considered in Chapter 2, for example, by suggesting that someone needn't think we can't be praised for morally required actions even if they think that in some sense, all such actions are non-voluntary.

That I make these kinds of claims might itself seem to be a kind of problem with the view that moral blackmail is a real phenomenon. We might think that there is a fundamental confusion here. Maybe it makes a metaphysical mistake about responsibility: it is either false that moral blackmail undermines responsibility, or it is true, but it can't be both at the same time. Maybe it also, or alternatively, makes a moral mistake: it would be wrong to hold people responsible in any way in the kinds of situations I've described.

The response to these worries is to observe that they presuppose a particular way of thinking about responsibility, which turns out to be at least unnecessary, and maybe also implausible, when examined explicitly. That presupposition is monism: there is a single property to which the term 'responsibility' invariably and univocally refers, and so my arguments so far – which have often involved saying that an individual can be responsible in some senses but not in others – are just confused.

The plausibility of my argument, that moral blackmail should be considered relevantly analogous to prudential coercion, therefore depends on whether we can resist this monistic view of responsibility. So, in this chapter

DOI: 10.4324/9781003259619-4

and the next, I set out a pluralistic theory which allows us to distinguish between different senses of responsibility. This has the happy consequence of vindicating the commonsensical things I've said so far about the effects of compulsion, prudential coercion, and moral blackmail. But (and I emphasise this at least in part to pre-empt the complaint that it is ad hoc to eschew monism about responsibility just because it is dialectically useful) there are strong independent reasons to think that this pluralistic theory is the right way to think about responsibility anyway.

I begin, in this chapter, by advocating a broadly functionalistic approach to the analysis of responsibility, distinguish between two functions that seem important – explanation and evaluation – and then explicate the concept of explanatory responsibility that arises from the first. In the next chapter, I discuss the more complex concept of evaluative responsibility, and then use both concepts to analyse more carefully the contrasts I drew in Chapter 1 between compulsion, coercion, and moral blackmail. By the end of Chapter 4, we will have a complete theory of responsibility which is pluralistic, rather than monistic. We will then be in a position to leave behind the worry articulated above about moral blackmail's individual responsibility ascriptions, as well as set up some of the puzzles about *collective* responsibility which I address in the final two chapters of this book.

3.1 Functions of Responsibility

The core of my proposal is as follows. In the spirit of recent broadly functional accounts of normative concepts – like Edward Craig's 'state of nature' analysis of knowledge,[1] Melissa Lane's similar approach to political obligation,[2] Bernard William's genealogy of truth and truthfulness,[3] and Miranda Fricker's 'paradigm-based explanation' of blame and forgiveness[4] – I propose to analyse the concept of responsibility by reflecting on what it distinctively adds to our practices when it appears. The meaning of 'responsibility' is settled by the functions that it plays in those practices.

My proposal is this: wherever responsibility crops up in a given practice, it is because the practice in question needs a way to ground some outcome by picking out a relation that holds between particular agents and events, by contrast with relations that are generic or universal. This need – for agent-specific groundings – arises in two main kinds of practices. First, it arises when we seek to *explain* states of affairs, and how an agent or their actions contributed to those things obtaining. Second, it arises when we seek to *evaluate* what are the normative upshots of states of affairs, and more specifically how an agent relates to a state of affairs (for example whether they intentionally caused it, though that doesn't always matter, and isn't the only thing that matters). So, there are two core concepts of responsibility, defined, respectively, by the functions they play in these two practices. An agent bears *explanatory responsibility* for a state of affairs when they or their actions play a crucial role in its explanation. An agent bears *evaluative responsibility* for a state of affairs when they stand in a relation to it that underpins some normative upshot specifically for them.[5]

These two core concepts then generate a range of particular conceptions of responsibility, depending upon our background theories (for example, of causation or punishment) and how we cash out the schematic elements that the core definitions contain. Sometimes these different conceptions will be rivals, for example, incompatible proposals for the one correct account of scientific explanation, but often they won't. So, we end up with a theory of responsibility that is both unified (since the functional analysis above exhausts what is meant by responsibility in whatsoever context it appears) and also pluralistic (insofar as it shows how multiple ways of understanding responsibility can be combined within the same theory).[6]

In this respect, my proposal is structurally similar to earlier analyses of the central political concepts of liberty and of rights, by Gerald MacCallum and Wesley Hohfeld, respectively.[7] MacCallum and Hohfeld offer schemes for diagnosing differences between people's assumptions about those concepts by analysing them as combinations of schematic elements which can then be explicitly scrutinised and identified separately. Recent work in both areas has explicitly sought to reinvigorate philosophical discussion by returning to, and developing, these tools of analysis.[8]

In the remainder of this chapter, and the next, I investigate responsibility by considering the role responsibility plays in the two practices sketched above: explanation and evaluation. (What I say in what follows will make clearer what I mean by those.) Unlike some of the methodological fellow-travellers listed above, I won't make any claims about how these practices emerged, about how universal they are, or about their relation to any putative basic human needs.[9] Nor will I claim that those practices incorporate the concept of responsibility as a matter of necessity: there can be (indeed, are) versions which don't. Rather, I just want to set out what comes to be possible once we incorporate responsibility into our conceptual apparatus. This will make greater sense of the claims made in Chapters 1 and 2 about the different effects on responsibility of compulsion and coercion, and about the parallels between prudential coercion and moral blackmail. It will also open up possibilities for some of the kinds of collective responsibility ascriptions which arise when (in Chapters 5 and 6) we consider moral blackmail in large political contexts.

3.2 Responsibility and Explanation

What do we do when we seek, and offer, explanations? What is the characteristic purpose of the activity of explaining? These are questions of long standing. Wesley Salmon's study of the history of scientific explanation suggests that they were live questions for the ancient Greeks:

> The search for scientific knowledge extends far back into antiquity. At some point in the past, at least by the time of Aristotle, philosophers

> recognized that a fundamental distinction should be drawn between two kinds of scientific knowledge — roughly, knowledge *that* and knowledge *why*. It is one thing to know *that* each planet periodically reverses the direction of its motion with respect to the background of fixed stars; it is quite a different matter to know *why*. Knowledge of the former type is descriptive; knowledge of the latter type is explanatory. It is explanatory knowledge that provides scientific understanding of the world.[10]

Setting aside the restriction to science, explanations are answers to questions about *why* (and, I might add, *how*). An explanation is an attempt to provide understanding. Presumably an explanation, for that reason, must be true. But not all true propositions are explanations, because not all of them provide understanding, by being a good answer to a why- or a how-question.[11]

Some answers to why- or how-questions are purely general in character. Someone might, for example, ask why planets have elliptical orbits. We would reply by citing Newton's laws of motion, or the suitably qualified versions thereof which are consistent with modern physics. Someone might ask how it is that we can always work out whether a number is a multiple of three by seeing whether the sum of its digits it is either three, six, or nine. We would reply by pointing to the features of the decimal number system that we use. Someone might ask why humans can talk but cats and dogs can't; we would answer them with some physiological facts about different kinds of mammal, including neurophysiological facts about their brains, and maybe some psychological facts as well.

These quite general answers to why- or how-questions would all be explanations in a perfectly familiar sense. However, not all explanations are like this. Sometimes, we seek explanations not for general truths but for particular ones. We ask questions like, 'Why is Mars moving like *that*?', or 'How come Jane just spoke to her cat and it didn't reply?' Replying to these with the purely general explanations given above will fall short. Besides Newton's laws of motion, and general claims about physiological differences between cats and humans, we also need to adduce particular facts (for example, about the mass and location of Mars, specifically, or about Jane's choices about how to behave when faced with cats).[12]

One concept of responsibility emerges when we recognise this need for particular explanations of a certain sort, namely those which crucially involve agents. Given that we are social beings such explanations are especially important for understanding our lives and environment. So, it makes sense that we might have a bespoke part of our conceptual apparatus to focus on them. The proposal under consideration is that this concept of responsibility is the thing that plays that role. Responsibility (in this sense) is the relation an agent bears to a state of affairs when they are a crucial part of its explanation: crucial in the sense that it will fail *as an explanation* if that relation isn't included, because what we end up with will not be useful for understanding what happens and why. For example, someone seeking to explain why this book was written will fail unless they say 'Ben wrote it'; my action is in this sense crucial to the explanation. On the present proposal, that being so is *just what it means* for me to be explanatorily responsible for this book's having been written.

It is useful to have a way of picking out an especially interesting and important kind of explanation. That is one advantage we get from the concept of explanatory responsibility, which we wouldn't have if we had only the concept of explanation. Another advantage is a degree of conceptual simplification. Explanations are, strictly speaking, relations between *propositions*: an explanandum (the proposition to be explained) and an explanans (the proposition or set thereof that does the explaining). However, talking in terms of propositions, even if it's correct, leads to tortuous and indirect ways of framing things. Using the language of *responsibility* is simpler and more direct, letting us identify explanatorily significant relations between agents and states of affairs (albeit that this way of defining responsibility means those relations in some sense depend on relations between the propositions in which those things feature). If I am right that we have good reason to pay especial attention to the class of explanations-involving-particular-propositions-about-agents, then it is useful for us to have the simpler conceptual apparatus afforded by the concept of evaluative responsibility.

This gives us the role which one concept of responsibility plays. To repeat: an agent bears explanatory responsibility for a state of affairs when *they* play a crucial role in explaining it. To return to my example above, if you ask 'Why does this book exist?' a satisfactory answer can't cite only general laws of physics and human behaviour, but also point to a special relation which *I* (but not others) bear to the relevant state of affairs; namely that I wrote this book. I am (explanatorily) responsible for it.

Putting it more carefully:

> *x* is explanatorily responsible for *y* just in case there exists some relation *Rxy* which plays a crucial role in the explanation of *y*.

The schematic letters here indicate places where we must offer further specification to generate a fully determinate conception of explanatory responsibility.

The variable *x* ranges over bearers of explanatory responsibility; that is, entities whose relations to states of affairs can play crucial explanatory roles. Assuming we accept the account given above that will mean *agents*, albeit that the range of the variable will be set differently depending on (for example) whether one thinks that only some types of agents can feature in genuine explanations, and what stance one takes on other types of entities, for instance, putatively collective agents like corporations or states.

The variable *y* ranges over *explananda*, states of affairs. We might sometimes want to talk of an agent having explanatory responsibility for something else, like a person or an object. For example, one might say 'Barbara is responsible for the sculpture', or 'Mr and Mrs Hepworth are responsible for

Barbara', and to mean those things to be explanations. However, on my analysis, when we say such things we implicitly have some specific states of affairs in mind, which could be made explicit: for example, we actually mean 'Barbara is responsible *for the sculpture's being made*', 'Mr and Mrs Hepworth are responsible *for Barbara's existence*', or 'for Barbara's artistic temperament', and so on.

The variable *R* ranges over relations between these entities. Disagreements concerning explanatory responsibility generally amount to disputes about what relation an agent must bear to a state of affairs to play a crucial role in its explanation. There are various familiar candidates from the philosophical literature: causation, free choice, intentional action, voluntary choice, counterfactual dependence, and so on. Working out which (if any) of these underpins explanatory responsibility is – though for obvious reasons not usually framed in the terms I'm proposing here – a central question in the philosophies of science and action. For example, our view about what relation really underwrites ascriptions of explanatory responsibility in science will depend, amongst other things, on whether we think scientific explanations are ultimately just hypotheses for generating empirical predictions, or rather that scientific inquiry attempts accurately to describe the basic causal structure of reality.[13] Upon this turns the question of whether finding a probabilistic correlation between two phenomena (as opposed to revealing a deterministic causal relation) is enough to say that one is (explanatorily) responsible for the other.[14]

There is no need for us to adjudicate these arguments. My point here is just that the parties to these disputes are, in effect, advocating different conceptions of explanatory responsibility falling under the core concept: that is, different relations which can play the appropriate role in our explanatory practices.[15] These disputes fall into a revealing pattern: a criterion for responsibility is proposed, then shot down by counterexamples, whose counter-intuitiveness consists in their implying ascriptions of responsibility that are explanatorily inadequate.[16] This pattern gives inductive support for my proposal that a conception of explanatory responsibility is successful only if it can play this role in our explanatory practices.[17]

My analysis offers a helpful diagnosis of what's at stake in disagreements about explanatory responsibility. For one thing, it shows that some such disagreements are illusory, because they advocate different conceptions which aren't necessarily rivals to each other. We might, for example, be pluralists about explanation,[18] and therefore think that someone might be explanatorily responsible for a state of affairs relative to one type of explanation, but not with respect to another. We might be contextualists about explanation, and hence think that the explanatory relation is different depending on the context, *explanans*, and *explanandum*.[19] The formal specification above helps with expressing that position. We can make claims about what one of the variables refers to *relative to* one of the other's being fixed. For example, we might say that explanatory responsibility involves (for example) voluntary action when we're talking about individual rational moral agents, but only counterfactual dependence when we're talking about children or adults with limited capacities.

In some cases, of course, disputes will continue, because the participants defend conceptions that are genuinely incompatible. In such cases, my analysis is less eirenic, but still illuminating, for two reasons. First, it will help to pinpoint the exact location of the disagreement: in rival views about what can count as *explanans* or *explanandum*, or (more frequently) in incompatible proposals for what relations are explanatorily crucial. Second, it suggests that there would be something circular about seeking to resolve these disputes merely by appealing to intuitions about the correct application of the concept of responsibility. Rather, we should concentrate on other matters, and ask: what does it mean to play 'a crucial role' in an explanation? What counts as genuine understanding? What is the relation between explanation and causation? Our stance on explanatory responsibility should be the consequence of such inquiries, not their starting point.

To conclude: one of our core concepts of responsibility arises from the need, internal to our practices of explanation, to express explanations which depend not on purely general laws and facts, but also upon how some particular entity relates to some particular state of affairs. I define the concept thus: *x* is explanatorily responsible for *y* just in case there exists some relation *Rxy* which plays a crucial role in the explanation of *y*. Particular conceptions of explanatory responsibility emerge when we set the range of the three variables here, and make use of what our background theories tell us about which relations are explanatorily crucial. Those conceptions may be rivals (in the sense that they represent alternative proposals for the 'true' account of explanatory responsibility in a given domain), but need not be.

This bears on our inquiry into moral blackmail because that is a phenomenon where – like prudential coercion, but unlike compulsion – the way that an individual's action is forced does not, I think, undermine their responsibility *in this sense*. If I am trying to explain why the highwayman ends up with my wallet, rather than me being dead, my choice can't help but be a crucial part of the explanation. If someone asks 'Why did Dastardly and Muttley win the race, rather than you?' then I won't adequately answer their question without saying that I exercised my moral agency to save the baby (and thereby throw the race). By contrast, if something comes about because someone physically compelled me to move in a given way, I (as an agent) am *not* crucial to the explanation, because the thing would have come about in just the same way if I had instead been unconscious, or a marionette.

Nevertheless, prudential coercion and moral blackmail plainly *do* undermine responsibility in other senses. In the next chapter, I move on to consider the second core concept of responsibility, and the myriad conceptions it engenders, and show how there is space to consider that they might be attacked even if explanatory responsibility is left intact.

Notes

1 E.J. Craig *Knowledge and the State of Nature*, Oxford: Oxford University Press, 1990. See also his 'The Practical Explication of Knowledge', *Proceedings of the Aristotelian Society* 87 (1986–1987): 211–226.
2 M. Lane 'States of Nature, Epistemic and Political', *Proceedings of the Aristotelian Society* 99 (1999): 211–224.
3 B. Williams *Truth and Truthfulness*, Princeton, NJ: Princeton University Press, 2002.
4 M. Fricker 'What's the Point of Blame? A Paradigm Based Explanation', *Noûs* 50 (2016): 165–183.
5 I expand on the idea of a 'normative upshot' below.
6 My distinction echoes other philosophers who have distinguished between different senses of responsibility, especially Ronald Dworkin, who distinguishes 'causal' from 'consequential' responsibility (R. Dworkin *Sovereign Virtue*, Cambridge, MA: Harvard University Press, 2000: pp. 287–288), Thomas Scanlon, who distinguishes 'attributability' from 'substantive responsibility' (T. Scanlon *What We Owe to Each Other* (Cambridge, MA: Harvard University Press, 1998): Chapter 6). What I say in these chapters is consistent with Dworkin and Scanlon, but it also seems to me to supersede those distinctions by capturing and grounding what they were getting at in a clearer and more generally applicable form. The same goes for others who have drawn similar distinctions. See, e.g., G. Watson 'Two Faces of Responsibility', *Philosophical Topics* 24 (1996): 227–248; M. Oshana 'Ascriptions of Responsibility', *American Philosophical Quarterly* 34 (1997): 71–83; J.E. Roemer *Equality of Opportunity*, Cambridge MA: Harvard University Press, 1998: pp. 16–21; S. Hurley *Justice, Luck and Knowledge*, Cambridge, MA: Harvard University Press, 2003: pp. 24–28; G. Yaffe 'Indoctrination, Coercion, and Freedom of Will', *Philosophy and Phenomenological Research* 67 (2003): 335 n. 1; S. Olsaretti *Liberty, Desert and the Market*, Cambridge: Cambridge University Press, 2004: p. 158 and S. Olsaretti 'The Concept of Voluntariness – A Reply', *Journal of Political Philosophy* 16 (2008): pp. 117–118; A. Mason *Levelling the Playing Field*, New York: Oxford University Press, 2006: p. 162 n. 4; P. Vallentyne 'Brute Luck and Responsibility', *Politics, Philosophy & Economics* 7 (2008): 57–80, at 58–59; Z. Stemplowska 'Making Justice Sensitive to Responsibility', *Political Studies* 57 (2009): 237–259, at 239–240; C. Knight *Luck Egalitarianism: Equality, Responsibility, and Justice*, Edinburgh: Edinburgh University Press, 2009, pp. 171–172; and (implicitly) E. McTernan 'How to Be a Responsibility-Sensitive Egalitarian: From Metaphysics to Social Practice', *Political Studies* 64 (2016): 748–764, at 749 and 762 n. 1.
7 G. MacCallum 'Negative and Positive Freedom', *Philosophical Review* 76 (1967): 312–334; W. Hohfeld *Fundamental Legal Conceptions as Applied in Judicial Reasoning*, New Haven, CT: Yale, 1917.
8 Concerning rights, see e.g. M.H. Kramer, N.E. Simmonds & H. Steiner *A Debate Over Rights*, Oxford: Oxford University Press, 2000; L. Wenar 'The Nature of Rights', *Philosophy & Public Affairs* 33 (2005): 223–253; L. Wenar 'The Analysis of Rights', in H. Kramer, C. Grant, B. Colburn & A. Hatzistavrou eds. *The Legacy of H.L.A. Hart*, Oxford: Oxford University Press, 2008; and H. Steiner 'Are There Still Any Natural Rights?' in the same volume. Concerning liberty, see H. Steiner *An Essay on Rights*, Oxford: Blackwell, 1994; I. Carter *A Measure of Freedom*, New York: Oxford University Press, 1999; M.H. Kramer *The Quality of Freedom*, Oxford: Oxford University Press, 2003; and M. Garnett 'Ignorance, Incompetence, and the Concept of Liberty', *Journal of Political Philosophy* 15 (2007): 428–446.
9 Contrast e.g. Craig and Williams, whose explications, respectively, of knowledge and truth are based on the idea that this kind of argument can excavate 'a function in

relation to some very basic need' that both explain and justify the concept in question. B. Williams *Truth and Truthfulness*, Princeton, NJ: Princeton University Press, 2002: pp. 31–32, and cf. E.J. Craig *Knowledge and the State of Nature*, Oxford: Clarendon Press, 1990: p. 2.

10 W. Salmon *Four Decades of Scientific Explanation*, Minneapolis: University of Minnesota Press, 1989: p. 3.

11 This is why A causing B isn't sufficient for A's explaining B, and perhaps not necessary either. For discussion of this point see P. Lipton 'Causation and Explanation', in H. Beebee, C. Hitchcock & P. Menzies eds. *The Oxford Handbook of Causation*, Oxford: Oxford University Press, 1999: pp. 619–631, at 620–625.

12 This account of explanation is loosely drawn from Carl Hempel, though there are various elements of his view (e.g. his insistence that the *explanans* must contain both general laws and particular facts, and that it must deductively entail the *explanandum*) which I shan't endorse here. See C. Hempel *Aspects of Scientific Explanation and Other Essays in the Philosophy of Science*, New York: Free Press, 1965: pp. 331–496.

13 See e.g. B. Van Frassen *The Scientific Image,* Oxford: Oxford University Press, 1980; B. Van Frassen *The Empirical Stance*, New Haven, CT: Yale University Press, 2002; S. Psillos *Scientific Realism: How Science Tracks Truth*, London: Routledge, 1999; and A. Chakravartty *A Metaphysics for Scientific Realism*, Cambridge: Cambridge University Press, 2007.

14 See e.g. P. Lipton *Inference to the Best Explanation*, 2nd edition, London: Routledge, 2004; W. Salmon 'Why Ask 'Why'?' in his *Causality and Explanation*, Oxford: Oxford University Press, 1998; and S. Psillos *Causation and Explanation*, Cheshunt: Acumen, 2002.

15 That it is useful to frame things in these terms, for highlighting disagreements between conceptions and understanding what is at stake, is itself a third useful role that the concept of explanatory responsibility can play for us.

16 This seems to me, for example, the correct interpretation of Harry Frankfurt and Susan Hurley's arguments against understanding responsibility in terms (respectively) of counterfactual dependence and of causal connection. See H. Frankfurt 'Alternative Possibilities and Moral Responsibility', *Journal of Philosophy* 66 (1969): 829–839, and S. Hurley *Justice, Luck and Knowledge*, Cambridge, MA: Harvard University Press, 2003.

17 As Craig says, in his explication of knowledge, 'we can include amongst our *explananda* such facts as the various analyses of the concept of knowledge that philosophers have given, the fact that controversy about certain of their clauses seems difficult to resolve, the facts about the reactions to sceptical proposals like that of Descartes, and all this be it noted not instead of but as well as the 'extension' (or whatever can uncontroversially be found of it) on which the standard approach uniquely concentrates attention'. See E.J. Craig *Knowledge and the State of Nature*, Oxford: Clarendon Press, 1990: p. 7.

18 E.g. C. Mantzavinos *Explanatory Pluralism*, Cambridge: Cambridge University Press, 2016; M. Lange *Because without Cause: Non-Causal Explanations in Science and Mathematics*, Oxford: Oxford University Press, 2017; C. Pincock 'Accommodating Explanatory Pluralism' in A. Reutlinger & J. Saatsi eds. *Explanation Beyond Causation: Philosophical Perspectives on Non-Causal Explanations*, Oxford: Oxford University Press, 2018: pp. 39–56.

19 James Woodward develops what I am calling a contextualist view about explanatory responsibility, albeit that he doesn't put it in those terms. See J. Woodward *Making Things Happen: A Theory of Causal Explanation*, Oxford: Oxford University Press, 2003.

4 Evaluative Responsibility

The previous chapter introduced the idea of a functional analysis of responsibility, which understands the meaning of the term to come from the role it plays for us in important practices. I proposed the following analysis: responsibility crops up wherever a given practice needs a way to ground an instance within that practice (for example an ascription, or an evaluation, or an outcome) by picking out a relation that holds between particular agents and events, by contrast with facts that are generic or universal. I went on to consider one such practice – explanation – and to elucidate the concept of (explanatory) responsibility which arises there: an agent is explanatorily responsible for a state of affairs just in case there exists a relation between them which plays a crucial role in the latter's explanation.

In this chapter, I go on to discuss a second practice or set of practices: evaluating what are the normative (not explanatory) upshots of how an agent is situated relative to a state of affairs. These two concepts of responsibility are orthogonal. Someone might be explanatorily responsible for something that happens without being evaluatively responsible in all or any senses. That is, in fact, one of the things that happens in the individual cases of prudential coercion and moral blackmail introduced in Chapter 1. It is also possible that someone might be evaluatively responsible because of how they are placed vis-à-vis a state of affairs without being explanatorily responsible for it. That feature – that we can be held responsible for what we do not control, to borrow Zofia Stemplowska's turn of phrase[1] – is also present in cases of moral blackmail (but not, I think, prudential coercion). It is crucial for understanding the large-scale manifestations of moral blackmail that we will go on to consider in Chapters 5 and 6.

In what follows, I begin by explaining the concept of evaluative responsibility, and the plurality of conceptions it encompasses once we recognise that different normative upshots might be grounded in different particular relations between agents and states of affairs. I conclude by using this theory of responsibility to think more carefully about the contrasts between compulsion, coercion, and blackmail that I introduced at the start of the book.

DOI: 10.4324/9781003259619-5

4.1 Responsibility and Evaluation

The project of explanation, though obviously relevant and important for action, has primarily to do with what we should believe, rather than how we should act. Other practices have more directly to do with action. We exhort, persuade, command, and offer reasons to each other to behave in certain ways. We assess each other's conduct, both on its own terms and also with a view to working out what we should, shouldn't, may or may not do next. We engage in a wide variety of practices, all of which might loosely be called 'evaluative'. Once again, I think we can excavate a concept of responsibility by reflecting on what type of expressive apparatus we might want as part of these evaluative practices.

Depending on our background moral theory, and the part of our moral practices under consideration, some of the things we say as part of those practices will have a wholly general character. This is so, for example, when Mill states the central principle of his utilitarianism:

> actions are right in proportion as they tend to promote happiness, wrong as they tend to produce the reverse of happiness.[2]

It is also so when Kant says that every agent should think:

> I ought never to act except in such a way that I could also will that my maxim should become a universal law.[3]

These general claims have particular implications, of course. They imply, respectively, that *I* must *now* act so as to maximise happiness, or that *I* must *now* ensure that my maxim in acting passes the test of the Categorical Imperative. But they do so only in the sense that the purely general explanations discussed in Chapter 3 did: they can be applied to particular cases, but do not refer ineliminably to any such cases for their content.

As before, then, we would suffer an expressive limitation if we were capable of articulating these things only in purely general terms. It may be that that limitation is appropriate, for example, because (following Kant, at least on some readings) we think that no genuine moral reason can depend on facts about particular people or circumstances. But many moral practices don't accept that expressive limitation, because they make claims that are grounded in something which has some particular elements as well as general. So, for example, when a judge proposes to punish a convicted criminal, they do something that would ordinarily be unacceptable (for it's not normally acceptable to incarcerate people, or take away their money, even if we call it a 'fine') and they justify it by pointing to something *that* criminal did in particular. When we praise someone for a kind act, it is the fact that *they* were the actor that merits praise. When you exhort me to keep a promise, you appeal not just to a general principle about promise-keeping, but also to the fact that *I* promised. If I fail to follow through you point to that particular fact about me to ground your criticism.

The point here is not that we should assume that instances like this are always (or ever!) justified, but just to observe something about the expressive resources they presuppose. Many of our moral practices require some conceptual apparatus that can capture the way that some grounding is done not solely by general principles but also (or instead) by how some particular individual agent is situated, relative to a particular state of affairs. My proposal is that this role picks out another core concept of responsibility, once again functionally defined, this time in terms of what its addition lets us do in our evaluative practices.

It isn't wholly easy to know how to label this concept of responsibility. One possibility would be 'moral responsibility', but this seems inapposite because other people have used that term to refer to particular conceptions falling under the more general concept I want to capture.[4] Another would be 'normative responsibility', but this seems inapt because it implies that 'explanatory responsibility' isn't normative; since I think that explanation is a normative project, I want to avoid that implication. I propose to call it *evaluative responsibility*, because it has to do with evaluating what follows from how a specific agent is situated.

As is clear from the preceding discussion, evaluative responsibility is a relation, that someone can bear to a state of affairs, which has some normative significance. To put it more generally, and to mirror the definition of explanatory responsibility in the previous chapter:

> x is evaluatively responsible for y, in respect of a normative upshot z, just in case there exists some relation Rxy such that z depends upon Rxy.

As before, x is an agent, and y is a state of affairs. The z variable ranges over 'normative upshots', by which I mean claims about what x must, may, or may not do; or about what some others must, may, or may not do in respect of x. The term 'normative upshot' is deliberately broad. It will cover both claims about conduct ('x should be punished', 'x should be compensated', 'x will decide what happens next') and claims about appropriate assessment ('x should be blamed', 'x should be praised').[5] By dependence, I mean what I have so far more loosely called 'grounding': pointing to the relation is sufficient to explain why the normative upshot obtains, and all else being equal the upshot wouldn't obtain if the relation didn't.

The relational variable R ranges over the relations between agents and states of affairs that ground these normative upshots. There are many different ways that one might set a range for this variable, and this means that the range of possible conceptions is wider than was the case with explanatory responsibility. It will be worth giving some examples, to make the point clear.

Some theories imply that there is just a single relation *R* that can ground evaluative responsibility, in respect of any upshot whatsoever (or, more plausibly, a very extensive range which is then taken to capture the only ones that matter). For example, consider a libertarian of Robert Nozick's stripe, who believes that everyone has a set of inviolable general rights *qua* rational agent, and that further special rights and duties arise just in case individuals freely consent to them.[6] Though he doesn't put it in these terms, Nozick's position implies the following conception of evaluative responsibility: agents are evaluatively responsible just when they have special rights and duties that have arisen from their free consent. The variable *z*, which represents normative upshots, ranges over all Hohfeldian molecular rights.[7] And the variable *R* is limited to one relation, namely that of free consent: my freely consenting is sufficient to change the Hohfeldian incidents (by giving away a claim, perhaps, or undertaking a duty) and it is also necessary, because nothing else (including, famously, claims of patterned distributive justice) will do.

Other theories pick out some particular normative upshot, and then specify a particular relation upon which it depends. So, for example, Hillel Steiner asks when an individual suffering some comparative disadvantage might lack a claim for it to be compensated; he answers that it is when the disadvantage is one which he caused freely, in the sense that 'others have not prevented him from doing otherwise'.[8] Steiner takes a normative upshot (an agent's lacking a claim to compensation which someone would ordinarily have in the circumstances) and makes a claim about what relation grounds it (the agent having freely caused that state of affairs). Steiner, in effect, says this: evaluative responsibility, specifically in respect of compensation, depends on free causal involvement. His claim is only about what grounds that specific normative upshot, and is silent with regard to any others, by contrast to Nozick's more general commitment as described above.

This second stance on evaluative responsibility, whereby its ascriptions are (perhaps implicitly) relativised to particular normative upshots, gives us the space for a wide pluralism about evaluative responsibility. Different normative outcomes can depend on different relations between individual agents and states of affairs, and what is necessary and sufficient for substantive responsibility in one domain need not be so everywhere else. In the law, for example, in different situations, there are different standards of culpability.[9] This might at first appear inconsistent, but in fact it isn't: rather, we can identify several different coexisting conceptions of evaluative responsibility applying to different types of crimes and punishments.

To give another example of pluralism about responsibility: Olsaretti echoes Williams in arguing that the appropriateness of praising or blaming an agent for an action depends on whether the action was 'intentional in the relevant respect and … to the extent that the agent deliberated, is the product of that deliberation',[10] but also says that whether or not an individual can claim compensation for disadvantages they suffer (for example, as a result of the operation of the market) depends on something else, namely whether those disadvantages arose through voluntary actions, in the sense explained in Chapter 1.[11] On my proposed taxonomy, Olsaretti's theory incorporates two different but consistent conceptions of evaluative responsibility.[12] With respect to some normative upshots (meriting praise or blame) the relevant relation is that of having intentionally and deliberately produced an outcome. With respect to some other normative upshots (having a claim to compensation for a disadvantage), the relevant relation is that of having produced that outcome voluntarily.[13]

I noted that pluralism of this sort is possible when we think about explanatory responsibility, but that it depends on some substantive philosophical views that one might disagree with (namely, some sort of pluralism or contextualism about explanation). I make a stronger claim here: there are good reasons to think that pluralism about conceptions of evaluative responsibility is true, or at any rate the default position.

First, consider the feature I've just mentioned. On my view, each ascription of evaluative responsibility must be (explicitly or implicitly) relative to particular normative upshots, or sets thereof. The monist position is not unintelligible (after all, above I suggested that Nozick's view of rights is very close to this), but it bears a burden of proof: the monist must argue that exactly the same relation between agents and states of affairs will ground every single possible normative upshot, including all the different upshots given in examples so far (praise, blame, punishment, reward, and all the rest). We would need some strong positive reason to think that such diverse normative upshots will all be grounded in the same way.

Second, the opponent of pluralism would need to show that a monist conception of evaluative responsibility is nevertheless able to play the role in our evaluative practices which gives it its purpose and content, namely to capture normative upshots that depend on particular relations between individuals and states of affairs, rather than wholly general principles. One might think that expressive need (which, if I am right, explains why we have this concept in the first place) pushes us away from the kind of Procrustean conception being imagined here. A moral practice augmented by *this* monist conception of evaluative responsibility is scarcely more expressively rich than one without.

Third, pluralism gives much the best fit to the everyday practices of evaluation which give the concept its function. We frequently combine different conceptions of evaluative responsibility in our moral thinking, even if we don't always think of it in those terms. So, for example, I am evaluatively responsible for this book's existence, in at least two ways. My having agreed to write it has placed an obligation on me to make the book exist, such that my publisher would have had a legitimate complaint against me if that state of affairs hadn't obtained; and my having successfully written it means that I am properly held to account (praised, blamed, paid, or punished) for its content. In other words, we have two different relations (x consented to produce y, and *x* successfully produced *y*), grounding two different upshots (*x* became vulnerable to complaint, and *x* became apt for praise or blame), but in each case following the pattern set out by the general definition of evaluative responsibility above.

For all these reasons, I think someone who accepts this way of thinking about responsibility will be likely to accept pluralism about evaluative responsibility, and agree that different normative upshots can depend on different relations between agents and states of affairs.

Nevertheless, most of the arguments in this book will be acceptable to someone who rejects pluralism and will still stand even if someone discharges the argumentative burdens I've just enumerated. The monist can accept my functionalist approach to analysing responsibility, the distinction between the concepts of explanatory and evaluative responsibility, and my definitions of both. They can also accept my diagnosis in Chapter 1 of the different effects on responsibility of prudential coercion, moral blackmail and compulsion, and the extension of the concept of moral blackmail to the collective contexts I discuss in Chapters 5 and 6. So, while pluralism about evaluative responsibility seems to me like a good fit with the other ideas discussed here, it isn't essential for the purposes of this book.

As well as being (probably) pluralistic, this theory of evaluative responsibility is in different senses both proliferative and reductive. It is proliferative in the sense that many moral and political theories turn out to deploy conceptions of evaluative responsibility even if they don't use the word. That is so whenever, in fact, they take some agent-specific normative upshot to be grounded by how that agent is situated. A lot of things which mightn't *seem* to be about responsibility, and certainly aren't framed in those terms, will turn out to be so if I am correct.

This may seem like a cost, but I tend to think it isn't. My aim has never been to take for a granted an intuitive extension for the concept of responsibility and find necessary and sufficient conditions which capture it exactly. As Chapters 5 and 6 will make clear, I think that this aspect of my theory is supported by the fact that it is useful and illuminating to consider those related practices in the same way as we do practices which are explicitly framed in terms of responsibility.

My theory is reductive in that an ascription of evaluative responsibility is never in itself capable of doing independent justificatory work. The concept of evaluative responsibility indicates a certain pattern of justification, namely an appeal to the normative import of how an agent is related to a state of affairs. An ascription of evaluative responsibility is an indication that one thinks a justification of that type is in the offing, but it is not itself such a justification. The real work must be done in showing that the relation asserted or implied does indeed do the necessary normative work, and that must be established by other means (for example, by arguing that punishment is merited by *actus reus* and *mens rea*, to take a legal example).

Since many legal, political and moral theories *do* treat ascriptions of responsibility as free-standing justifications, this aspect of my proposal is quite radical indeed, and might once again seem like a heavy cost. Nevertheless it seems to me inevitable if we think that responsibility is indeed a concept defined by its functional roles, and if we think that I have come at all close to describing those roles accurately. In other words, a reader who has otherwise found what I have said here persuasive should for that reason bite the bullet and accept its reductive implication, that an ascription of evaluative responsibility is a yet-to-be-fulfilled promise that a justification with a particular structure is available.

4.2 Compulsion, Coercion, and Blackmail

The theory of responsibility developed in these two chapters helps us make better sense of the mechanisms of force discussed and distinguished in Chapter 1. Compulsion, prudential coercion and moral blackmail are all ways that an agent can be made to do something. Nevertheless, they work in different ways, that can be captured by their different implications for the victim's responsibility in the senses we are now in a position to distinguish properly.

Physical compulsion undermines responsibility in both core senses. It precludes explanatory responsibility, because someone's choices as an agent aren't crucial to the explanation of what happens if they are effectively treated as a marionette. Compulsion also precludes evaluative responsibility in multiple senses: that someone's body is used by someone else to achieve certain ends means they don't (for example) merit either praise or blame for what happened, and leaves them perhaps deserving compensation for any comparative disadvantages that arise.

In cases of prudential coercion, things are different. Coercion does not preclude explanatory responsibility, because *how they choose to respond to the threat* will always be a crucial part of the explanation of what happens. But – at least on the views of coercion discussed in Chapter 1 – coercion *does* undermine evaluative responsibility in a number of senses, for example because a victim of coercion doesn't deserve blame for what they are coerced into doing, or because they can't justly be held liable for the consequences of coerced acts.

Moral blackmail, the phenomenon I introduced in Chapter 1, is very much like prudential coercion in these respects. If we are explaining how things go when someone is morally blackmailed, it is crucial to refer to how that agent chooses to respond to the morally charged situation they face. So, explanatory responsibility is not diminished. But, as discussed in Chapter 1, many of the reasons to think coercion undermines what we can now identify as *evaluative* responsibility also apply here, though, as we'll see shortly, it's more complicated in these cases.

So, the effect of moral blackmail, as with prudential coercion, is to pull responsibility in these different senses out of alignment.

In fact, with moral blackmail (as opposed to prudential coercion), this happens in multiple different ways, because in a case of moral blackmail the real diagnosis of what happens involves an agent's relation to at least two different states of affairs, and involves distinguishing multiple different conceptions of evaluative responsibility.

The first state of affairs – and the one I've been talking about so far – is what they are blackmailed into producing. In the Wacky Races example from Chapter 1 this is *their losing the race*. With regard to this state of affairs, they are explanatorily responsible. They are not evaluatively responsible in at least some senses, for example those to do with liability to compensation or punishment. Consider: would you punish the protagonist if their throwing the race represented a breach of contract? I assume not. Further, would you entertain a claim for compensation or insurance if they destroyed valuable belongings in the course of saving the baby from the pond? It doesn't seem out of the question. Those intuitions depend on it being plausible that evaluative responsibility on the relevant conceptions is undermined.

Nevertheless, plausibly here – and this marks a departure from prudential coercion – we might think the agent retains some evaluative responsibility for their losing the race. We might, for example, praise them for saving the baby at cost to themselves, depending on whether or not we think someone deserves praise or blame for morally obligatory acts.

The second state of affairs to which the morally blackmailed agent bears responsibility relations, I think, is the one which constitutes their being morally blackmailed in the first place. In the Wacky Races example, this is *the baby's being in the pond*. It might seem strange to think that *this* is a state of affairs the agent is responsible for: it was after all Dastardly and Muttley who manufactured it, rather than the protagonist. But with our new theory of responsibility in hand we can see that this is only part of the full picture. It's true that the protagonist is not *explanatorily* responsible for the baby's plight. But, nevertheless, their relation to that state of affairs – namely that they are its sole occupant with the ability to rescue the baby – *does* ground normative upshots for them, specifically that they are under a duty to save the baby (even at the cost of throwing the race). In other words, they are *evaluatively* responsible for that state of affairs, in at least two senses: by dint of their relation to it they come to be under a duty they didn't have before, and they will be liable for censure if they choose not to discharge that duty. That is, in a nutshell, exactly what their being morally blackmailed *means*.

Moral blackmail therefore involves multiple fractures between our concepts of responsibility and their subsidiary conceptions. With respect to the state of affairs the agent is morally blackmailed into producing they are explanatorily responsible without being evaluatively responsible in all senses; with respect to the state of affairs which constitutes the blackmail they are in some senses evaluatively responsible without being explanatorily responsible.

To conclude: our second core concept of responsibility arises from the need, internal to our moral, political, and legal practices, to identify ways that normative upshots (praise, blame, reward, punishment, compensation, and so on) depend upon the particular relations between agents and states of affairs. I define the concept thus: x is evaluatively responsible for y, in respect of a normative upshot z, just in case there exists some relation Rxy such that z depends upon Rxy. As with the concept of explanatory responsibility discussed in Chapter 3, particular conceptions of evaluative responsibility emerge when we set the range of these four variables, especially by focusing on specific normative upshots and identifying which relations between agents and states of affairs those upshots depend on. Those need not be the same, at least as far as the concept of evaluative responsibility determines, and probably won't be: this way of thinking about responsibility lends itself to pluralism about the different relations that ground different normative upshots.

This concludes our discussion of the concepts of responsibility. It also allows us to better understand what happens (and what happens differently) in cases of compulsion, coercion, and moral blackmail. In particular, it excavates the interesting structure of that last phenomenon. Cases of moral blackmail are analogous to cases of prudential coercion, but more complex because they involve relations to two different states of affairs, with different implications for explanatory and evaluative responsibility depending on each of those relations. To return to and expand Stemplowska's way of putting it,[14] the victim of moral blackmail is *simultaneously* (evaluatively) responsible for a situation they don't control (explain), and control (explain) a situation for which they're not (evaluatively) responsible.

Notes

1 Z. Stemplowska 'Holding People Responsible for What They Do Not Control', *Philosophy, Politics & Economics* 7 (2008): 355–377.

2 J.S. Mill *Utilitarianism*. Ed. G. Sher, Indianapolis, IN: Hackett, 2001: p. 27.

3 I. Kant *Grundlegung zur Metaphysik der Sitten*, originally published 1785. Ed. & trans. M. Gregor as *Groundwork of the Metaphysics of Morals*, Cambridge: Cambridge University Press, 1994: p. 15.

4 Olsaretti, for example, in 'The Concept of Voluntariness – A Reply', *Journal of Political Philosophy* 16 (2008): 117–118.

5 Actually I think that even apparently detached evaluative judgements like praise and blame are best thought of practically, as species of conduct. I shan't argue the point here, but see e.g. Fricker 'The Relativism of Blame and William's Relativism of Distance', *Proceedings of the Aristotelian Society Supplementary Volume* 84 (2010): 151–177; M. Fricker 'What's the Point of Blame? A Paradigm Based Explanation', *Noûs* 50 (2016): 165–183; and B. Williams 'Internal Reasons and the Obscurity of Blame' in his *Making Sense of Humanity, and Other Philosophical Papers*, Cambridge: Cambridge University Press, 1995: pp. 35–45.

6 R. Nozick *Anarchy, State and Utopia*, New York: Basic Books, 1974: p. 1.

7 W. Hohfeld *Fundamental Legal Conceptions as Applied in Judicial Reasoning*, New Haven: Yale University Press, 1917. For a helpful gloss, see M.H. Kramer 'Rights without Trimmings', in M.H. Kramer, N.E. Simmonds & H. Steiner *A Debate Over Rights*, Oxford: Oxford University Press, 2000: pp. 7–112, at 7–59.

8 H. Steiner *An Essay on Rights*, Oxford: Blackwell, 1994: p. 216. In fact Steiner's conception is a little more complicated, since he adds the proviso that this all has to take place against a background of equal freedom. But the simplified version above is sufficient for my purposes, which is just to illustrate a point about the geometry of disagreements about conceptions of responsibility.

9 See e.g. essays in A. Simester ed. *Appraising Strict Liability*, Oxford: Oxford University Press, 2005; M.S. Moore 'The Strictness of Strict Liability', *Criminal Law and Philosophy* 12 (2018): 513–529; and D.O. Brink 'The Nature and Significance of Culpability', *Criminal Law and Philosophy* 13 (2019): 347–373.

10 S. Olsaretti *Liberty, Desert and the Market*, Cambridge: Cambridge University Press, 2004: p. 159, and B. Williams 'Voluntary Acts and Responsible Agents', *Oxford Journal of Legal Studies* 10 (1990): 1–10.

11 S. Olsaretti *Liberty, Desert and the Market*, Cambridge: Cambridge University Press, 2004: pp. 139–141.

12 Olsaretti herself discusses a distinction between two types of responsibility in her theory (*Liberty, Desert and the Market*, Cambridge: Cambridge University Press, 2004: pp. 152–161). The distinction she draws (between 'attributability and 'substantive responsibility') is one that she borrows from Scanlon, and – like Scanlon's – seems to me usefully disambiguated by being put in terms of the distinction I draw here.

13 In fact, Olsaretti's position has subsequently become more complicated than this, later arguing that whether or not one can be held evaluatively responsible for a disadvantageous state of affairs (in the sense of not meriting compensation for it) depends also on a 'theory of stakes': namely an account of how bad the possible disadvantages are. Voluntariness is thus a necessary, but not sufficient condition, on this conception of evaluative responsibility. In my terms, Olsaretti's proposal plays on limiting the variable *y*, which refers to states of affairs, depending on the badness of those states of affairs. See S. Olsaretti 'Responsibility and the Consequences of Choice', *Proceedings of the Aristotelian Society* 109 (2009): 165–188.

14 Z. Stemplowska 'Holding People Responsible for What They Do Not Control', *Philosophy, Politics & Economics* 7 (2008): 355–377.

5 Passing the Buck in Intergenerational Justice

In Chapters 1 and 2, I argued that moral blackmail is a real and normatively weighty phenomenon, and in Chapters 3 and 4 set out its underpinnings in a pluralistic theory of responsibility. By itself that might not be sufficient to persuade someone that moral blackmail is something useful to think about in moral and (especially) political philosophy. After all, my main example so far has been a fusion of a clichéd thought experiment and a children's cartoon. Even if moral blackmail isn't by definition either non-existent or all-pervasive, it might be trivial by dint of being a phenomenon not worth wasting our time on.

In the remainder of this book, I refute this charge of triviality by showing how the concept of moral blackmail can be put to useful work in two serious and difficult debates in political philosophy. In each case, the crux turns out to be a wide-scale instance of moral blackmail as I have defined it. Seeing that allows us to understand the cases more clearly, and also points the way to some solutions.

The payoff of these discussions is twofold. First, my view's having distinctive and clear implications is a vindication of the concept of moral blackmail as a tool of philosophical analysis. Second, I think that the implications I set out are also illuminating for those who are concerned with these two debates, regardless of their investment in the more foundational discussion with which I started.

In this chapter, I consider the first of these two political philosophical debates. It concerns intergenerational justice, and in particular what is wrong with 'buck passing', as Stephen Gardiner calls it. These are policies where one generation 'can secure benefits for itself by imposing costs on its successors, and avoid costs to itself by failing to benefit its successors'.[1] I begin by giving some examples of buck-passing, survey different attempts to capture exactly how to account for these diachronic wrongs, and show that none is wholly satisfactory. Then, I argue that intergenerational buck-passing is an instance of moral blackmail, albeit on a much larger social and temporal scale than the examples I've used so far. Understanding it this way allows us to explain and accommodate two central (but ostensibly incongruent) features

DOI: 10.4324/9781003259619-6

of these cases: first, that later generations have a legitimate complaint against their buck-passing predecessors, and second, that this complaint doesn't constitute an excuse not to discharge the (heavier than otherwise) duties they've been bequeathed. In line with what I said at the end of Chapter 4, they end up with substantial evaluative responsibilities arising from states of affairs for which they are not explanatorily responsible. This interpretation reconciles the most plausible features of both sides of this debate.

Understanding intergenerational buck-passing this way adds evidence to my case that moral blackmail is a real phenomenon and a useful analytic tool. It shows how the tool might be applied in a real case, giving a clear and persuasive answer to this vexed question, and hinting at a solution to the non-identity problem which Derek Parfit posed for population ethics.[2]

5.1 Buck-Passing and the Non-identity Problem

Suppose that we reflect on the failure of successive past generations to respond adequately to the threat of climate change, with the result that present and (especially) future generations must bear massive costs to avert catastrophe. Or, we consider domestic political policies which incur large national debts to pay for benefits to present citizens, where the burden of repayment will be borne by future citizens. Such policies aren't always wrong. It might be appropriate for a present generation to incur massive debt to head off some urgent threat, even if that debt imposes very significant burdens on future generations.[3] But oftentimes they seem to be wrong. Some of the reasons for thinking so might be synchronic, for example, because we think environmental harm is bad as such, or because profligacy is vicious. Most distinctively, though, these policies have a problematic diachronic aspect. They are bad for future generations, which might not yet be born, or might include individuals who are born but not yet the relevant agents for these political decisions.

Most people who write about generational buck-passing share the view that it is usually wrong, but there is no consensus about exactly how to capture the diachronic problem I've identified here. There are three main proposals in the literature: that it is harmful, that it violates rights, and that it is exploitative.

I begin with harm. One intuitive way to try to explain the wrongness of generational buck-passing is as follows. It is wrong, all else equal, to cause harm. The effects of buck-passing policies include harms which are done to the members of future generations. So, it is wrong, all else equal, to adopt those policies. Passing the buck on climate change means that many of our descendants will suffer extreme hunger or ill health through the spread of disease, or suffer in wars over scarce water resources, and so on. Incurring massive debt which must be repaid by future generations reduces the resources they will have for alleviating suffering and promoting welfare. These bad consequences are harms that will take place in the future, and that is – on this way of explaining it – by itself sufficient to show why it is wrong to pass the buck in the present.

The challenge posed to the harm-based account by Parfit is as follows.[4] It is crucial to our argument that we say future people are *harmed*, not just that bad things happen to them, for it is our policy's being harmful to those people that is supposed to show why it's wrong. Harm, so the argument goes, is a comparative and person-specific notion: someone is harmed by an action if it makes *them* worse off than *they would otherwise be*.[5] That imposes a constraint on when we can say harm has taken place. We must be able to consider two alternative ways the world might be, to identify some individual who is in some sense present in both alternatives, and then to note that they are worse off in one than the other. But this condition is threatened in the kind of case we are considering. The policy decisions we make about, for example, environmental action have a significant effect on who is and is not born: depending on what we do, different people will live and die, and those that live will likely make different procreative decisions at different times. The cumulative effect, so Parfit's argument implies, is that several generations down the line from our buck-passing actions there will be nobody alive who would have been alive had we not passed the buck. So, at the crucial moment where our buck-passing comes to bite, there will be nobody of whom it is true that *they* are worse off than they would otherwise be; *they* would not exist if we hadn't passed the buck. Hence, nobody is harmed, which means that harmfulness can't be why generational buck-passing is wrong.

The non-identity problem has provoked a vast literature which it would be tokenistic to try to summarise here.[6] It is also not clear that the problem succeeds in sinking the kinds of judgements in population ethics which are its target. So, my conclusion here is conditional. To the extent that one is worried about the non-identity problem, it will undermine the attempt to diagnose the wrongness of generational buck-passing in terms of its harming members of future generations. Of course, even if one isn't worried by the non-identity problem, there may still be some reason either to prefer the diagnosis in terms of moral blackmail that I offer below, or to regard it as identifying a new and distinct problem with buck-passing alongside the familiar harm-based account.

The element of the harm-based account of buck-passing which made it vulnerable to the non-identity problem was this: we need to be able to make counterfactual comparisons between possible worlds which are different enough to generate the kind of stark contrasts we need, but not so different as to disrupt the relations of identity or counterparthood between specific individuals whose situations we can compare. These two requirements plainly pull in different directions. The more one describes a future which is markedly worse as a result of our buck-passing, the less plausible it is to say that the individuals in those future generations are the same as (or direct counterparts of) those who would have existed if we had adopted a different policy. So, there seems no easy way out of the conundrum for someone who tries to explain the wrong of buck-passing by appealing to considerations of harm.

A very similar problem arises for the second account I consider, which is a diagnosis in terms of rights-violations. Shifting from talk of harm to talk of rights-violation is a move which has been made several times in the literature, often as an attempt to avoid the non-identity problem.[7] Applied to the case of generational buck-passing, the idea is that if we think any person has a right to, for example, a basic level of resources or opportunities, then buck-passing policies are wrong when (and because) they violate those rights for future people.

Despite its provenance in attempts to respond to Parfit, I am not convinced that the rights-based account marks an improvement over the harm-based account. For one thing, its scope is limited. There will be buck-passing policies which impose burdens on future generations but fall short of the kind of fundamental right-violation described above, for example if the buck-passed is a heavy but not crippling national debt. In such cases, this account would either have to say that buck-passing isn't wrong in those cases or concede that there must be something else which makes it wrong, either of which is an unsatisfactory manoeuvre given that the point was to offer a plausible and general diagnosis. For another, I worry that the rights-based account still falls foul of the non-identity problem, for reasons which echo an argument of Matthew Rendall's: unless we believe people are being made worse off in respect of some specified goods or protections than *they* would otherwise be, it is implausible to say that their rights in respect of those same goods and protections have been violated.[8] Once again, our entitlement to this kind of counterfactual judgement will be disrupted by the *ex hypothesi* profound procreative consequences of the buck-passing policies we are examining.

A third category of accounts focuses on the idea that generational buck-passing is in some sense unjust. Rendall himself suggests that the core problem with buck-passing is one of distributive justice: when we pass the buck we are misappropriating a benefit from future generations, and taking more than we deserve.[9] Wikfred Beckerman argues that it is unfair for a generation to take advantage of the fact that it happened to arrive earlier in time to use up supplies of critical natural capital.[10] Chris Bertram argues that buck-passing is *exploitative*: when adopting such a policy a 'precursor generation can set things up so that their own lack of contribution effectively precommits the labour of their successors'.[11]

We should, I think, reject Rendall and Beckerman's versions of this idea. They fare no better than their rivals against the non-identity problem, because they are still committed to the kinds of counterfactual comparisons which bedevil the harm- and rights-based accounts. When Beckerman speaks of 'using up critical natural capital',[12] he cannot simply mean just that there comes to be a smaller amount of natural capital available for future generations – that is probably in some sense always true – but that the amount that those generations have is less than *they* would otherwise have, as a result of our actions, which is the kind of judgement which looks like it's blocked.

The problem with Rendall's view is more subtle, but similar. When Rendall says that 'we [a buck-passing generation] are taking more than we deserve',[13] he must mean more than just that a buck-passing policy gives us more than a non-buck-passing policy would. That by itself wouldn't be sufficient to show that there was a wrong being done, because there can be innocuous instances where a policy leaves less than it otherwise might for future generations, for example when a present generation consumes only within its entitlements, or when it justifiably burns resources to avert some urgent present threat. Rather, Rendall must mean that we are taking more *at the unjust expense of* members of a future generation, which is to say that we are forcing an unjust distribution of resources across a diachronic population (just in the same way that a policy which gives disproportionate resources to only one racial group would be an unjust distribution across a synchronic population). The problem then is that there is no single diachronic population across which these two distributions can be compared, because – as in the more straightforward non-identity cases – the decisions we make affect who comes into existence. That means that, with regard to the distribution across the diachronic population created by our buck-passing decision, it looks as though that population could not enjoy a different distribution, or at least not one which is markedly different in respect of the key buck-passing policy, since otherwise different people would be born, and we would have a divergent diachronic population. In that case the reasoning of the non-identity problem implies that there can't be any injustice about the distribution *for that population*. So, the prospects for these alternative diagnoses of the wrongness of buck-passing once again look bleak.[14]

Turning now to Bertram, the problem recurs yet again if we understand 'precommitting the labour of their successors'[15] as a matter of the distribution of labour. However, it seems to me that Bertram is not in fact identifying a purported problem of distributive justice, but rather one of exploitation. Gardiner makes a similar point, albeit not in the same terms. He says we should understand buck-passing as a sort of extortion.[16] If we adopt such a policy, our actions (for example, failing to act early to avert catastrophic climate change) create a situation for our successors where they face the threat of awful circumstances unless they act in particular ways (for example, by performing the – now presumably much more onerous – actions required to avert the disaster that we could have averted at a lesser cost). Describing it as a case of *extortion* doesn't seem quite right to me – after all, for reasons I've already explained it's a mistake to think that there's anything being *transferred* from some later generation to us – but, like Bertram's evocation of the language of exploitation, it indicates that something wrong is going on. And Gardiner's diagnosis of what is wrong with extortion – that it shows disrespect, that it has wider social costs by eroding the bases of just cooperative schemes, and that it is 'a threat to how we see ourselves, morally speaking'[17] – is very persuasive. The problem with buck-passing is that it is an attack on agency or (maybe more controversially) autonomy. It is in this sense that (to return to Bertram's phrase) it 'precommits the labour of [our] successors',[18] and this is why it is wrong.

Bertram and Gardiner's diagnoses are persuasive, but they lack a firm theoretical underpinning to explain exactly how this extortion or exploitation takes place. My proposal is that we should draw on the resources developed in Chapter 1 and say that what happens in cases of buck-passing is, in effect, that members of future generations are *morally blackmailed*, and that this problematic relationship is what is being picked out less exactly by the language of extortion and exploitation.

5.2 Buck-Passing as Moral Blackmail

My proposal, then, is that buck-passing is (usually) problematic because it is an instance of large-scale moral blackmail. The way that buck-passing 'pre-commits'[19] is by pushing future generations into non-voluntary action: it creates a situation where members of a future generation must act in a particular way to avoid unacceptable alternatives. It is in virtue of this that it is exploitative or extortionate.[20]

In some cases of buck-passing, the alternatives faced by the later generation will be prudentially unacceptable. That will be the case when past inaction on climate change means that a present generation now faces the choice between very expensive action and ruinous natural disaster. That is already true now, in some parts of the world.[21] But in other cases the burden which generational buck-passing imposes is not a prudential one, or not just a prudential one. There exist intermediate generations who are downstream of the first crucial buck-passing decisions, but who are upstream of the consequences which trigger dire prudential peril. For such generations the burden is moral: as a result of past inaction, they have a duty to incur grave costs to avert disaster for future generations. What has happened is that they have, effectively, been morally blackmailed. Admittedly, and by contrast with the cartoon case considered in Chapter 1, there is no specific perpetrator who intentionally designs the policy so that it has this effect on them in particular. But moral blackmail is defined in terms of its effects on the character of the choices forced on the victim. In this respect, and in respect of the problematic effects on their autonomy and responsibility, the parallel is exact. The impersonal moral blackmail perpetrated by buck-passing precludes voluntary choice in just the same way as the impersonal prudential force exerted by the free market, to draw a parallel with Olsaretti's argument against Nozick.[22]

Understanding generational buck-passing as moral blackmail explains and reconciles two features of an intermediate generation's predicament which might otherwise seem to be in tension. The successors of a buck-passing generation have been wronged, even if they don't themselves (now) face prudential catastrophe. Being morally blackmailed is prima facie bad. It is an attack on one's ability to exercise voluntary agency, and it imposes costs one didn't choose. If we find ourselves in this position, then we have a legitimate complaint against their buck-passing predecessors. But, crucially, this doesn't absolve present persons of their responsibilities. The duties created are genuine, and we would do wrong to simply pass them on like a Ponzi scheme. Even if we didn't choose to be in the situation, our relation to it has weighty normative upshots. How can our being wronged in this situation not act as an excuse regarding the forward-looking duties? How can we reconcile the apparently contradictory judgements of responsibility involved?

Seeing that this is a case of moral blackmail lets us see how. Our having been wronged just consists in our having been put in a situation where those duties press on us, and make all alternatives morally unacceptable.[23] This has the effect of prising apart the plural judgements of responsibility that apply to us. To put it in terms of the theory of responsibility developed in Chapters 3 and 4, the result of buck-passing is that a later generation is *evaluatively* responsible (in the sense of bearing the costs) for a state of affairs for which they are not *explanatorily* responsible (because they didn't choose it).

For these reasons, I think that the most plausible diagnosis of what is wrong with generational buck-passing is that it undermines voluntary action, and in most cases it does so through moral blackmail, rather than through prudential coercion. This diagnosis captures and reconciles various important features of the relevant cases. I have focused almost exclusively on the environment in this discussion, but I think the same things can be said about the case of national debt I mentioned earlier.

Diagnosing buck-passing as moral blackmail also allows us to evade the non-identity problem. The problem with the harm- and rights-based accounts was that the purported diagnosis of how some future individual had been wronged depended on a counterfactual judgement about whether *they* are worse off than they would otherwise have been. Identifying that someone has been morally blackmailed is dependent on no such counterfactual judgements. It depends only on a claim about what duties they are under – which is entirely forward-looking, and not based on any tricky counterfactuals at all – and on the explanation for how they come to be under that duty, which is by that point a straightforward matter of historical record, without the proleptic uncertainty which the non-identity problem hinges on. It is still true that the people so burdened would not have existed without the actions of the buck-passing generation. But our judgement that they are burdened does not – unlike the other arguments considered above – depend on comparing how things would have been different *for them*.

It is unlikely that someone worried by the non-identity problem is going to be wholly satisfied at this point. They might, for example, say that my sketch of a solution here leaves untouched a more fundamental problem, which is that the non-identity problem also challenges the view that there was in the first place a duty to act (and which the earlier buck-passing generation failed to discharge). Doesn't positing a duty to (for example) intervene early to avert catastrophic climate change depend on thinking that doing otherwise would harm future generations?[24]

Discussion of the non-identity problem tends to address this challenge by trying to account for that original duty in other ways, as indeed Parfit does when he speaks of the need to develop a non-person-affecting Principle of Beneficence.[25] That line of response poses my view an apparent dilemma. If it is successful, then it identifies what the original generation did wrong without needing to appeal to moral blackmail; if it isn't successful, then the non-identity problem remains a problem which the theory of moral blackmail doesn't solve. Either way, my central aim in this chapter – to provide proof-in-use of my theory – is undermined.

In fact, my proof-in-use survives whether or not these attempts to develop non-person-affecting principles work.

Consider first what follows if they are successful. My analysis in terms of moral blackmail doesn't seek to identify everything that is wrong about the earlier generation's policy, but just what is specifically wrong about its being a buck-passing policy. It is compatible with many views about why a duty arises in the first place, claiming only that a distinct wrong is done if a generation simply passes the duty on. So, a non-person-affecting Principle of Beneficence which successfully explains the former is no problem for my view, and will likely (for the reasons already given in this chapter) anyway need to adopt my theory of moral blackmail to explain the latter.

On the other hand, the failure of those attempts wouldn't be a problem either. The objection is that the non-identity problem undermines the duty which the earlier generation supposedly had and then shirked. If that objection stands, then many apparent cases of buck-passing are merely apparent, because in many such cases there is in fact no buck to be passed. That would mean that the puzzle of buck-passing is less widespread and interesting than we might have thought, but not that my theory is any less of a solution to it. My claim is just that buck-passing, when (and howsoever often) it arises, it is best analysed as an instance of moral blackmail, including because – unlike its rivals – that analysis solves the non-identity problem at least as it applies to the wrongness of the original duty being transferred to successor generations.

This sketch of a solution to the non-identity problem is not the only reason to accept that generational buck-passing is an instance of moral blackmail. Nevertheless, my theory's promising a potential way to sidestep the non-identity problem is a further consideration in its favour, at least for those who are concerned about that argument in population ethics.

To conclude: in this chapter, I have put my theory of moral blackmail to use by showing that it offers a novel analysis of intergenerational buck-passing which is more plausible than its rivals, in particular by avoiding (and maybe even hinting at a general solution to) Parfit's non-identity problem. Most importantly, this analysis highlights and explains the central features of buck-passing cases. The later person who is faced with heavy burdens as a result of earlier policy failures has a serious and legitimate complaint about the situation they've been put in, but at the same time that complaint doesn't (as we might normally expect) excuse them the duty to discharge those burdens, because the grounds of the complaint – the reason it is indeed legitimate – is that they have genuinely come to be under that onerous duty. They have come to be evaluatively responsible for a state of affairs which some others, not them, are explanatorily responsible for. Understanding buck-passing as moral blackmail simultaneously explains why it's wrong, and how it works.

Notes

1 S.M. Gardiner 'Accepting Collective Responsibility for the Future', *Journal of Practical Ethics* 5 (2017): 22–52, at 24.

2 D. Parfit *Reasons and Persons*, Oxford: Oxford University Press, 1984: pp. 351–380.

3 Admittedly, most instances of permissible (or required) buck-passing depend for their apparent defensibility on there being a benefit for members of future generations too, as when governments borrow to establish important infrastructure, or to defend against an existential threat of war or pandemic. But we can imagine that there might be some cases where that benefit is clearly not sufficient to outweigh the burden of debt, and yet the benefit to present people might be sufficient to make the buck-passing policy right, all things considered.

4 D. Parfit *Reasons and Persons*, Oxford: Oxford University Press, 1984: pp. 351–380.

5 I set aside what we might measure when deciding if someone is 'worse off', except to observe that I think the problems in the previous paragraph – pestilence, war, famine or death – are clearly the sorts of things that will count as doing so on any plausible proposal.

6 M.A. Roberts 'The Nonidentity Problem', in E.N. Zalta & U. Nodeman eds. *The Stanford Encyclopedia of Philosophy*, Winter 2022 edition. https://plato.stanford.edu/archives/win2022/entries/nonidentity-problem/ [accessed 11 March 2024].

7 See e.g. J. Woodward 'The Non-Identity Problem', *Ethics* 96 (1986): 804–831; D. Smolkin 'Toward a Rights-Based Solution to the Non-Identity Problem', *Journal of Social Philosophy* 30 (1999): 193–208; and L.H. Meyer & D. Rose 'Enough for the Future' in A. Gosseries & L.H. Meyer eds. *Intergenerational Justice*, Oxford: Oxford University Press, 2009: pp. 219–248.

8 M. Rendall 'Non-Identity, Sufficiency and Exploitation', *Journal of Political Philosophy* 19 (2011): 229–247, at 230. Rendall's version of the argument doesn't specify that the comparison and the purported rights-violation are in respect of the same goods or protections, which means that he is vulnerable to the familiar argument that one can be wronged, or have one's right violated, without being harmed. That argument is potent but is a red herring here, since in intergenerational cases the rights we are most concerned about are protections against devastating harms; hence my tweak to make clear that this isn't a way to defend the rights-based account of the wrongness of buck-passing.

9 M. Rendall 'Non-Identity, Sufficiency and Exploitation', *Journal of Political Philosophy* 19 (2011): 236–242.

10 W. Beckerman 'Intergenerational Equity and the Environment', *Journal of Political Philosophy* 5 (1997): 395–405, at 402.

11 C. Bertram 'Exploitation and International Justice', *Imprints* 10 (2007): 69–92, at 81.

12 W. Beckerman 'Intergenerational Equity and the Environment', *Journal of Political Philosophy* 5 (1997): 395–405.

13 M. Rendall 'Non-Identity, Sufficiency and Exploitation', *Journal of Political Philosophy* 19 (2011): 236.

14 Much depends here on one's attitude to the non-identity problem. Someone who is antecedently convinced that it isn't a problem will be unmoved by all the preceding arguments. And someone who is antecedently convinced of some of the proposals here (that we can harm members of future generations, violate their rights, or deal with them unjustly) could treat these conclusions as reductiones ad absurdum, at least as long as they don't also deploy the non-identity problem against their rivals, as e.g. Rendall does ('Non-Identity, Sufficiency and Exploitation', *Journal of Political Philosophy* 19 (2011): 229–230). A reader who takes one of those lines will probably not think that the alternative accounts of the wrongness of buck-passing have been eliminated. But, as I noted above, they might nevertheless think that my moral blackmail-based account is persuasive on its own terms, either on its own or as a distinct element of the wrongness of such policies.

15 C. Bertram 'Exploitation and International Justice', *Imprints* 10 (2007): 70.

16 S.M. Gardiner 'The Threat of Intergenerational Extortion: On the Temptation to Become the Climate Mafia, Masquerading as an Intergenerational Robin Hood', *Canadian Journal of Philosophy* 47 (2017): 368–394.

17 S.M. Gardiner 'The Threat of Intergenerational Extortion: On the Temptation to Become the Climate Mafia, Masquerading as an Intergenerational Robin Hood', *Canadian Journal of Philosophy* 47 (2017): 375.

18 C. Bertram 'Exploitation and International Justice', *Imprints* 10 (2007): 70.

19 C. Bertram 'Exploitation and International Justice', *Imprints* 10 (2007): 395–405.

20 C. Bertram 'Exploitation and International Justice', *Imprints* 10 (2007): 395–405; S.M. Gardiner 'The Threat of Intergenerational Extortion: On the Temptation to Become the Climate Mafia, Masquerading as an Intergenerational Robin Hood', *Canadian Journal of Philosophy* 47 (2017): 368–394.

21 IPPC *Climate Change 2022: Impacts, Adaptation, and Vulnerability*. Contribution of Working Group II to the Sixth Assessment Report of the Intergovernmental Panel on Climate Change. Eds. H.-O. Pörtner et al., Cambridge: Cambridge University Press, 2022.

22 S. Olsaretti *Liberty, Desert and the Market*, Cambridge: Cambridge University Press, 2004: p. 150.

23 In this I differ from Gardiner, for whom showing that buck-passing is extortative – or undermines voluntariness, in my terms – is a reason to reject the purported obligations that are borne by later generations ('The Threat of Intergenerational Extortion: On the Temptation to Become the Climate Mafia, Masquerading as an Intergenerational Robin Hood', *Canadian Journal of Philosophy* 47 (2017)). Even if we ignore the independent reasons for rejecting that conclusion, we might think that it is self-defeating for Gardiner, since it eliminates the very feature which was on his terms supposed to show that something wrongful was happening.

24 My thanks to an anonymous referee for raising this worry.

25 D. Parfit *Reasons and Persons*, Oxford: Oxford University Press, 1984: pp. 378–379.

6 Taking Up the Slack in Global Justice

In this chapter, I turn to the second application of my theory of moral blackmail. As in the preceding discussion of intergenerational justice, my aim here is twofold: to offer a new solution to a familiar problem, and thereby also to lend some proof in use of the account I set out in Chapter 1.

The problem I consider here is whether, in a context requiring collective action, the failure of some agents to comply with their individual duties can generate further duties for others, including those who (at first, anyway) did everything they were required to: duties to 'take up the slack', in David Miller's phrase.[1] Drawing on my account of moral blackmail, I offer a new argument that people do have a duty to take up the slack. Unlike other arguments for that conclusion, I accept the most powerful intuition on the other side, which is that compliers are wronged in situations of partial compliance. The point is just that the best explanation of that intuition – that compliers have been morally blackmailed – implies that they nevertheless do indeed come to be under a duty to take up the slack.

6.1 Problems of Partial Compliance

The problem I have in mind applies, I think, to any situation where there is partial compliance with collective duties. However, philosophical discussion of this debate takes place mostly in the context of global justice, and I think it is there that the practical implications are most vivid. So, I take that as my test case in what follows.

Here is the problem. There exist many people in the world who are in dire need, which is to say that their basic needs (for example, for water, shelter, and security) are unmet. Assume, for the sake of argument, that this fact generates a duty for those who aren't in dire need.[2] In an ideal world, every such duty-bearer will fulfil their fair share of the burden, and dire need will be eliminated. However, in our non-ideal world, what is likely to happen is this: some agents comply with their duties, and some don't. The result is that dire need persists.[3] In these circumstances, we can ask: do the compliers have a

DOI: 10.4324/9781003259619-7

duty to do more than what was originally their fair share? Do they have a duty to take up the slack?

There are various ways someone might argue against the duty to take up the slack. These include Liam Murphy's argument that one mistakes the structure of the collective duty if one thinks that the size of someone's share can change depending on other people's non-compliance;[4] Miller and L.J. Cohen's complaints that it is straightforwardly counterintuitive to think we can come under further duties as a result of others shirking theirs;[5] Cohen's argument that accepting the duty would have 'disastrous consequences';[6] and Murphy and Miller's contention that taking up the slack would mean failing to treat non-compliers as responsible moral agents.[7]

Zofia Stemplowksa has considered each of these arguments and, in each case, identified decisive problems for the argument in question.[8] Against Murphy, she argues that 'unfairness alone is never sufficient to invalidate enforceable duties to aid', because 'duties … are not lifted off our shoulders simply because we may weigh wrongly the relevant moral weights on each side and therefore conclude that the duties are too heavy for us to bear'.[9] Against Miller and Cohen, Stemplowska argues that the intuitive considerations they appeal to merely show that 'there are some wrongs such that there is no positive duty of justice for third parties to correct them', rather than that there are no such wrongs at all, and she adduces intuitive considerations, at least as powerful as Miller and Cohen's, that there are at least some wrongs of this kind, to demonstrate that the appeal to intuitions can't be a reason to reject the duty.[10] Stemplowska argues that Cohen overstates the likelihood of disaster if people accept a duty to take up the slack, and concludes that the most his argument delivers is a warning 'that popularizing and implementing the duty in some specific circumstances might be ill-advised'.[11] Finally Stemplowska responds to Murphy and Miller's view that taking up the slack means treating non-compliers as though they're not responsible by making a point which aligns with what I have said here in Chapters 3 and 4. Their argument, she says, is guilty of 'conflating two senses of responsibility':

> anticipating failure means that we are not seeing agents as responsible in the sense of well-behaved, but we could still recognize them as responsible in the sense of having the capacity to act responsibly and fulfil their duties.[12]

Each of Stemplowska's arguments seems to me decisive. Given their individual force, one might have imagined that, cumulatively, they would comprise a powerful inductive refutation of the opponent of the duty to take up the slack. That is not, however, how things frequently go. This position remains widespread, and is for its proponents interestingly durable in the face of what ought to be compelling opposition.[13]

The reason for that durability, I think, is that in fact those detailed arguments – though no doubt offered sincerely – aren't the real *motivation* for the opponent of the duty to take up the slack. The real motivation is the intuitive appeal that their view holds, that there would be something wrong – indeed outrageous! – in holding the complier liable for further burdens resulting from the failures of their fellows. If that intuitive appeal really is the driver here, then Stemplowska's case-by-case refutation – powerful though it is – is unlikely to settle the matter. After all, her opponent can correctly point out that her inductive strategy doesn't preclude someone coming up with a new argument which her existing arguments don't defeat, and if someone is intuitively convinced of the conclusion, they will for that reason be convinced that there must be some such argument that isn't vulnerable to Stemplowska's points.

Here is a different strategy, complementary to Stemplowska's. My starting point is to concede the intuitive power of Stemplowska's opponents' view, and agree with them that there is something morally outrageous about the duty to take up the slack. The question is: what does that intuition prove?

The opponent of the duty to take up the slack relies, I think, on an implicit abductive inference: the idea is that we take the intuition as given, recognise that the best explanation for that intuition is that we should be opposed to the duty to take up the slack, and endorse it accordingly.

My strategy in what follows disrupts this inference by presenting a different explanation for our intuitions, namely that these cases – like the intergenerational cases considered in Chapter 5 – are instances of large-scale moral blackmail. Other people's non-compliance puts compliers in a position where they are forced to take further burdensome action, because not to do so would be genuinely morally unacceptable. Perhaps non-compliers don't have this effect in mind, at least not this effect on specific compliers. But, for the reasons given in Chapter 5, that isn't important for deciding whether the complier's subsequent decision is morally blackmailed, or for demonstrating the complex resulting effects on the complier's responsibilities.

At the very least, the presence of that rival candidate explanation disrupts the rationale for opposing the duty to take up the slack. The implicit assumption that such opposition is the *best* explanation for our intuitions now stands in need of justification. Even the reader who remains sceptical about the idea of moral blackmail might agree that the *possibility* of an explanation of this sort shifts the burden of proof to the opponent rather than the proponent of the duty to take up the slack.

In fact, though, I think my argument goes further than this. I show that our (on the face of it conflicting) intuitions can be explained and vindicated by the broader account of moral blackmail and responsibility developed in this book. This seems to me not just a *possible* explanation, but a *good* explanation, and a better one than its rival. So, by the abductive reasoning which – if I am correct – underpins opposition to the duty to take up the slack, we can in fact prove that there *is* such a duty. This is not the only argument in favour of the duty to take up the slack – I think there remain powerful reasons to accept all the arguments of Stemplowksa's that I surveyed above – but it offers a novel way to break the dialectical deadlock. Its doing so, in turn, offers further vindication of my theory of moral blackmail, by demonstrating its usefulness as a tool of analysis in complex cases like this.

6.2 Moral Blackmail and Taking Up the Slack

The view that we have no duty to take up the slack has its intuitive appeal, I think, because it offers a way to combine two attractive thoughts, each of which is prima facie plausible, but which apparently sit in tension. The existence of people suffering dire need *does* generate duties for those who aren't in that position, but also, the weight of those duties for individuals is manageable and limited in scope. This promises a middle way between the Scylla of libertarianism, which denies that dire need generates any duties at all,[14] and the Charybdis of strict act-utilitarianism, which implies that it generates duties which might in principle be massively demanding for ordinary individuals.[15]

This aim – to show that rejecting the libertarian position needn't entail something as demanding as full-blown act-utilitarianism – plainly motivates many of the people who have argued against the duty to take up the slack (or for restricted versions of consequentialism which incorporate similar mechanisms).[16] To the extent that people argue for this position (rather than just relying on the fact that it would be congenial if true), they tend to say something of the following form: we shouldn't think that compliers have a duty to do more than their fair share, because they would be wronged thereby. Or, to put it another way, because the complier would have a correct complaint (either a complaint directly against the non-complier, or maybe just a general claim for compensation) we shouldn't take them to be under the duty.

My view is that the basic claim being made here is correct. The complier is indeed wronged in these situations.[17] But *that* isn't a reason to think that they don't come to be under a duty to take up the slack. In fact, it's the opposite.

The testing ground for my strategy is one prominent set of arguments, based on an appeal to the complier's autonomy. In some cases, these are arguments which Stemplowska didn't consider; in others, they represent ways her opponents might alter the emphasis of their views so that they are less vulnerable to the arguments she makes. These are not the only arguments which we might consider – below, I show how my analysis can be extended to, for example, those which appeal to unfairness in the distribution of burdens – but my point is made most clearly by focusing for now on these. Each is a variation of the same basic thought: the complier has a correct complaint because their autonomy is infringed by the duty to do more than their fair share, and that shows that they should not, in fact, be taken to be under that duty.

Exactly how this infringement of autonomy comes about is rarely argued for, and some considerable interpretative footwork is needed to make it at all credible. Many of the things the relevant philosophers say about autonomy turn out to be unsatisfactory on closer inspection. Some (Brock, for example) argue as though it is the purported duty itself which constrains our autonomy.[18] So construed, the argument can't work. To begin with, if duties of beneficence *per se* restrict our autonomy, then an argument like this proves too much: the original duty to do one's fair share will be ruled out on the same grounds, since it too is such that we have only one permissible action open to us. So, this line of thought won't help us find stable ground between libertarianism and act-utilitarianism.

Even setting this worry aside, the basic claim being made – that duties constrain one's autonomy – is problematic. Much depends on what we mean by 'autonomy', just as was the case when (in Chapter 1) we explored the different reasons why coercion might undermine autonomy. On the one hand, we might mean the concept as it appears in Kant's moral philosophy, in which autonomy is a property of the will which is governed only by laws which it gives to itself.[19] Because this amounts to acting on duty, on Kant's view there can be no duty which conflicts with autonomy, but (for the same reason) saying that there is no duty to take up the slack because that would constrain autonomy (in this sense) would merely reiterate the central claim, rather than argue for it. On the other hand, we might understand autonomy to be an individual ideal whose protection or promotion is a political aim, as (for example) Raz, Gerald Dworkin or Oshana have argued.[20] But at first sight it makes no difference to one's individual autonomy what duties one is under, either because that has nothing to do with instantiating the ideal[21] or because those duties act as a parameter on what would count as the autonomous life.[22] Of course, compliers' autonomy might be infringed if we were to use state coercion to *force* them to do more than their fair share, but the question at hand is not *whether the complier should be forced to do more than their fair share*, but rather *whether the complier comes to be under a duty* so to do, and whether *that* diminishes their autonomy.

My analysis of moral blackmail shows how – the challenges indicated above notwithstanding – it *can* harm someone's autonomy to come to be under the duty to take up the slack. Under the kinds of circumstances we are considering, non-compliance puts a complier in a situation where the moral reasons demand that they act in a way which requires a sacrifice which they'd not make were it not for their having been placed in that situation. Other people's non-compliance has made the alternatives to their sacrifice morally unacceptable. So, they cannot act voluntarily, and this attacks their autonomy.

Depending on one's favoured view of autonomy, the details may work out differently. I start by offering a detailed diagnosis of the situation in terms of my own theory of autonomy, but I also show below that similar conclusions can be reached by those who favour other ways of understanding it.

On my view, the autonomous life is one where one decides for oneself what is valuable and lives one's life in accordance with that decision.[23] That latter clause is captured by a responsibility condition: someone's life is autonomous to the extent that their life goes in accordance with their decisions about what is valuable, and they are responsible for the fact. I understand this way of thinking about autonomy to be within the same tradition as John Stuart Mill's ideal of individuality,[24] and Raz's conception of autonomy as 'self-authorship'.[25] This is what Oshana calls an *externalist* conception of autonomy: autonomy consists not only in intrinsic states of the individual, but also in extrinsic relations.[26] Raz himself didn't put this in terms of responsibility – he talked more loosely about how the autonomous individual 'is one who *makes* his own life' [my emphasis][27] – but, as I have argued elsewhere, construing this as a responsibility condition of the kind I defend is the best way of making sense of this distinctive aspect of self-authorship.[28]

Moral blackmail is a problem for autonomy for various reasons.[29] Most importantly, it undermines responsibility, in the ways described in Chapter 4. Someone who is morally blackmailed suffers impaired responsibility in at least two ways.

With respect to the present state of affairs which constitutes the moral blackmail, for example the baby's being in the pond, or (to return to the example in Chapter 5) present generations' finding themselves with the burden of rectifying past generations' buck-passing, the agents are not explanatorily responsible, and yet they *are* evaluatively responsible in the sense that they bear heavy moral burdens by dint of how they relate to that state of affairs. The racer is the sole possible rescuer, so they must save the baby at the cost of losing the race; present generations have a final chance to rectify past generations' mistakes, so we must undertake onerous policy changes to mitigate the prudential harm to future generations. To the extent that discharging those duties has a substantial impact on how their life goes, their autonomy is impaired by these impacts being ones for which they weren't explanatorily responsible.

In addition, with respect to the future state of affairs which constitutes their discharging their responsibilities, the victim of moral blackmail is explanatorily responsible – it's the racer's choice which explains why the baby is saved, it's (hopefully) present generations' efforts which explain why climate change is mitigated – and yet not wholly evaluatively responsible, because of how they were boxed in by the character of their choices. To put it in Raz's terms, there will be a prominent episode in their life of which they aren't the author.

So, on my way of thinking about autonomy, the ways that moral blackmail undercuts responsibility on my pluralistic theory will all impair individual autonomy. I've focused here on explaining it in those terms, but I think similar things can be said about other conceptions of autonomy too, which means this conclusion isn't dependent on the reader accepting my favoured way of understanding that value. So, for example – and here I echo the reasons given in Chapter 1 for thinking that *coercion* is generally a problem for autonomy – one might think moral blackmail is a problem for autonomy because it creates an oppressive relation between the blackmailer and their victim,[30] or because it controls or limits meaningful choice,[31] or because it introduces disharmony in one's motivational hierarchy.[32] Even though philosophers diverge on how to understand autonomy, they can converge on the conclusion that moral blackmail is bad for it.

Returning now to the question of partial compliance, the preceding reasoning shows why the opponents of the duty to take up the slack have identified a genuine wrong suffered by compliers. The actions of non-compliers effectively morally blackmail compliers, thereby undermining their autonomy. The problem is that this diagnosis – which gives a non-question-begging reason to accept opponents' core intuition – gives the lie to the conclusion which they draw. Someone is morally blackmailed only if they genuinely come to be under the relevant constraining moral reasons, for – *ex hypothesi* – they are not literally being compelled or coerced to take up the slack. So, the complaint only holds if others' non-compliance genuinely does bring a complier under the duty to take up the slack, which is to say if the answer to the question I posed at the start of this chapter is 'yes'.

I have focused here on those who explain the core intuition in terms of a cost to autonomy, but the crucial part of my argument is the observation that these are cases where someone is morally blackmailed because they genuinely come to be in a situation where the alternatives are all morally unacceptable. One could think that while thinking that the original intuitive resistance to the duty to take up the slack should be grounded in something different. For that reason, a structurally similar point can be made against appeals to unfairness, or inequitably distributed responsibility.[33]

These arguments come in different forms. One might argue against the duty to take up the slack on the grounds that the complier has a correct complaint through having been put in an unfair situation, or having been needless burdened, or having been given someone else's responsibility. Put this way, the arguments are problematic for the same reason as explained above, because they presuppose what they seek to refute. The complaints in question (that the complier is treated unfairly, or needlessly burdened, or unjustly made responsible) are correct only if we genuinely do think that the complier comes to be under the duty to take up the slack.[34]

Alternatively, someone might construe this as a reductio ad absurdum of the duty to take up the slack. If there were such a duty, so the argument goes, then it would lead to unfairness, or needless burden, or unjust distribution of responsibilities. So, we shouldn't take compliers to be under that duty in the first place.[35] This way of understanding the argument isn't vulnerable to the charge of self-defeat outlined in respect of the simpler versions considered above. But it nevertheless comes at a cost, because the considerations brought to bear then look like they backfire. We want to say not only that compliers *would* be treated unfairly, or inequitably, or have their autonomy infringed, *if* we were to believe in the duty to take up the slack, but that as a matter of fact they *do* suffer these wrongs as a result of their fellows' non-compliance. The independent intuitive plausibility of that latter claim was precisely what the opponents of the duty were relying upon.[36] So, we should think the complier comes to be under that (complaint-generating) duty, which is to say that they are morally blackmailed.

So, once again, the concept of moral blackmail has proved its analytic use. Once we see that it is in play, we can identify a new and more powerful argument for the duty to take up the slack in situations of partial compliance, grounded in the very reasons people offer for opposing that duty. Whether condemned for strict self-contradiction or self-defeat of this looser sort, because they turn out to evoke the phenomenon of moral blackmail the arguments offered for answering 'No' actually motivate exactly the opposite.

To conclude: in this chapter, I have put my theory of moral blackmail to a second test, by showing how it gives a distinctive and satisfying solution to the problem of partial compliance in global justice. Other solutions to that problem fail to account for both of the key data which explain why the problem is interesting and difficult. First, the complier who potentially faces heavier burdens as the result of their peers' non-compliance has a legitimate complaint against them, of a sort which would usually generate an excuse, or suggest that they have no further duties. But, second, if others' needs were dire enough in the first place to generate burdens at all, then this will continue to happen if those dire needs aren't met because some people don't comply with their responsibilities. Understanding this as a situation of moral blackmail justifies and reconciles these two ostensibly inconsistent claims. The complier has a legitimate complaint against the non-complier because the latter's inaction has morally blackmailed the former. But of course that complaint exactly involves accepting that the complier genuinely has come to be under those onerous duties. They end up evaluatively responsible despite not being explanatorily responsible for their peers' moral failure.

Like my discussion of intergenerational buck-passing in Chapter 5, I think this suggests two things about the account of moral blackmail that I have developed in this book. First, its usefulness in exploring and resolving this debate in global justice is a kind of proof-in-use of the ideas I have developed. Second, although I have focused here mostly on the duty to take up the slack in one domain, namely duties of global justice to alleviate dire need, the reasoning clearly generalises to any situation involving collective responsibilities with which there is only partial compliance. Those situations will, presumably, be very common. So, this should be a final and decisive reassurance to the sceptical reader who worried that moral blackmail is a phenomenon which arises only in the context of philosophical thought experiments and children's cartoons. Depending on how prevalent partial compliance really is, it seems like moral blackmail is something we potentially suffer, and perpetrate, all the time.

Notes

1 D. Miller 'Taking Up the Slack? Responsibility and Justice in Situations of Partial Compliance', in C. Knight & Z. Stemplowska eds. *Responsibility and Distributive Justice,* New York: Oxford University Press, 2011: pp. 230–245.

2 Liam Murphy characterises this as a situation where there is a collective duty, borne by the set of individuals who aren't in dire need, which generates derivative individual duties for the members of that set. See L. Murphy *Moral Demands in Nonideal Theory*, New York: Oxford University Press, 2000. One needn't follow Murphy in framing the problem in terms of collective duties, though: one could simply think that all individuals are under a duty to do their part in relieving the problem.

3 I set aside for now the question *why* not all agents comply with their duties; it might be because those duties are as a matter of fact unenforced, or practically unenforceable, or because we think as a matter of principle that they aren't enforceable because they are e.g. duties of benevolence rather than justice. For helpful discussion of these different positions, see e.g. B. Barry 'Humanity and Justice in Global Perspective', in J.R. Pennick ed. *NOMOS 24: Ethics, Economics, and the Law*, New York: New York University Press, 1982: pp. 219–252; A. Buchanan 'Justice and Charity', *Ethics* 97 (1987): 558–575, at 559; S. Loriaux 'Beneficence and Distributive Justice in a Globalising World', *Global Society* 20 (2006), 251–265, at 253–256; and L. Valentini *Justice in a Globalized World: A Normative Framework*, New York: Oxford University Press, 2011: pp. 6–8.

4 L. Murphy *Moral Demands in Nonideal Theory*, New York: Oxford University Press, 2000.

5 D. Miller 'Taking Up the Slack? Responsibility and Justice in Situations of Partial Compliance', in C. Knight & Z. Stemplowska eds. *Responsibility and Distributive Justice*, New York: Oxford University Press, 2011: pp. 242–243; L.J. Cohen 'Who Is Starving Whom?', *Theoria* 2 (1981): 76.

6 L.J. Cohen 'Who Is Starving Whom?', *Theoria* 2 (1981): 73, 80.

7 D. Miller 'Taking Up the Slack? Responsibility and Justice in Situations of Partial Compliance', in C. Knight & Z. Stemplowska eds. *Responsibility and Distributive Justice*, New York: Oxford University Press, 2011: p. 241; L. Murphy *Moral Demands in Nonideal Theory*, New York: Oxford University Press, 2000: p. 113.

8 Z. Stemplowska 'Doing More Than One's Fair Share', *Critical Review of International Social and Political Philosophy* 19 (2016): 591–608. For other arguments to this end – which I think are equally powerful, and I fear equally unable to persuade their opponents, see e.g. D. Owen 'Refugees, Fairness and Taking up the Slack', *Moral Philosophy and Politics* 3 (2016): 141–164.

9 Z. Stemplowska 'Doing More Than One's Fair Share', *Critical Review of International Social and Political Philosophy* 19 (2016): 596–598.

10 Z. Stemplowska 'Doing More Than One's Fair Share', *Critical Review of International Social and Political Philosophy* 19 (2016): 598–599.

11 Z. Stemplowska 'Doing More Than One's Fair Share', *Critical Review of International Social and Political Philosophy* 19 (2016): 599–601.

12 Z. Stemplowska 'Doing More Than One's Fair Share', *Critical Review of International Social and Political Philosophy* 19 (2016): 601–602.

13 I give further examples of this durability in the next section.

14 E.g. R. Nozick *Anarchy, State and Utopia*, New York: Basic Books, 1974, especially Chapters 7 & 8; J. Narveson 'Welfare and Wealth: Poverty and Justice in Today's World', *The Journal of Ethics* 8 (2004): 305–348.

15 E.g. P. Singer 'Famine, Affluence and Morality', *Philosophy & Public Affairs* 1 (1972): 229–243; S. Kagan *The Limits of Morality*, Oxford: Clarendon Press 1989; and P. Unger *Living High and Letting Die*, New York: Oxford University Press, 1996.

16 E.g. E. Ashford 'The Demandingness of Scanlon's Contractualism', *Ethics* 113 (2003): 273–302; L.J. Cohen 'Who Is Starving Whom?', *Theoria* 2 (1981): 65-81; B. Hooker 'Rule-Consequentialism, Incoherence, Fairness', *Proceedings of the Aristotelian Society* 95 (1994): 19–35; L. Murphy *Moral Demands in Nonideal Theory*, New York: Oxford University Press, 2000; and M. Ridge 'Fairness and

Non-Compliance', in B. Feltham & J. Cottingham eds. *Partiality and Impartiality: Morality, Special Relationships, and the Wider World,* Oxford: Oxford University Press, 2010: pp.194-222.

17 It seems likely that Stemplowska would accept this too, incidentally; my thanks to an anonymous referee for pointing this out.

18 E.g. D. Brock 'Defending Moral Options', *Philosophy & Phenomenological Research* 51 (1991): 909–931; R.H. Myers 'The Inescapability of Moral Reasons', *Philosophy and Phenomenological Research* 59 (1999): 281–307; A. Rajczi 'The Argument from Self-Creation: A Refutation of Act-Consequentialism and a Defence of Moral Options', *American Philosophical Quarterly* 48 (2011): 315–332.

19 I. Kant *Grundlegung zur Metaphysik der Sitten*, originally published 1785. Ed. & trans. by M. Gregor as *Groundwork of the Metaphysics of Morals*, Cambridge: Cambridge University Press, 1994.

20 G. Dworkin *The Theory and Practice of Autonomy*, Cambridge: Cambridge University Press, 1988; M. Oshana *Personal Autonomy in Society*, Aldershot: Ashgate, 2006; J. Raz *The Morality of Freedom*, Oxford: Clarendon Press, 1986.

21 As, for example, on Gerald Dworkin's view that autonomy consists in higher-order endorsement under conditions of procedural independence, which – since it consists just in internal facts about the relations between one's preferences – is insensitive to the duties one is under. See G. Dworkin *The Theory and Practice of Autonomy*, Cambridge: Cambridge University Press, 1988: Chapters 1 & 2.

22 As, for example, on Oshana's view, where standing in just relations to one's co-citizens is a necessary condition of autonomy (M. Oshana *Personal Autonomy in Society*, Aldershot: Ashgate, 2006: pp. 86–90); and maybe also on Ronald Dworkin's view, if we understand his challenge model of ethics as depicting an ideal of autonomy, albeit not under that name, since duties of justice towards co-citizens are part of what defines (but therefore does not restrict) the good life (R. Dworkin *Sovereign Virtue*, Cambridge, MA: Harvard University Press, 2000: pp. 237–284).

23 B. Colburn *Autonomy and Liberalism*, New York: Routledge, 2010: pp. 21–42.

24 J.S Mill *On Liberty*, originally published 1859, reprinted in *On Liberty and Other Writings*, ed. S. Collini, Cambridge: Cambridge University Press, 1989: at pp. 56–74.

25 J. Raz *The Morality of Freedom*, Oxford: Clarendon Press, 1986: pp. 369–399.

26 M. Oshana *Personal Autonomy in Society*, Aldershot: Ashgate, 2006: pp. 1–20. This is by contrast to someone like Gerald Dworkin, on whose view autonomy consists just in one's desires being structured a certain way, regardless of whether they are satisfied (G. Dworkin *The Theory and Practice of Autonomy*, Cambridge: Cambridge University Press, 1988: Chapters 1 & 2).

27 J. Raz *The Morality of Freedom*, Oxford: Clarendon Press, 1986: p. 375.

28 B. Colburn 'In Defence of Comprehensive Liberalism', *Philosophy and Public Issues* 2 (2012): 17–29, and 'Autonomy and End of Life Decisions – A Paradox' in J. Räikkä & J. Varelius eds. *Adaptation and Autonomy: Sour Grapes in Life and Death Choices*, New York: Springer, 2013: pp. 69–80.

29 B. Colburn *Autonomy and Liberalism*, New York: Routledge, 2010: pp. 74–88; S. Olsaretti *Liberty, Desert and the Market*, Cambridge: Cambridge University Press, 2004: p. 137 and passim. There are of course reasons other than a cost to autonomy to think that non-voluntary action is bad. One might think so on the basis of an entirely non-autonomy-based concern for consent or individual rights, as Olsaretti notes (S. Olsaretti *Liberty, Desert and the Market*, Cambridge: Cambridge University Press, 2004: p. 104).

30 For example, on the view of autonomy in M. Oshana *Personal Autonomy in Society*, Aldershot: Ashgate, 2006.

31 For example, on the view of autonomy in T. Beauchamp & J.F. Childress *Principles of Biomedical Ethics* (5th edition), New York: Oxford University Press, 2001.

32 For example, on the view of autonomy in H. Frankfurt 'Freedom of the Will and the Concept of a Person', *Journal of Philosophy* 68 (1971): 5–20 and and G. Dworkin *The Theory and Practice of Autonomy*, Cambridge: Cambridge University Press, 1988.

33 Amongst those who argue against the duty to take up the slack on the basis of unfairness are Ashford ('The Demandingness of Scanlon's Contractualism', *Ethics* 113 (2003): 273–302), Hooker ('Rule-Consequentialism, Incoherence, Fairness', *Proceedings of the Aristotelian Society* 95 (1994): 19–35), Murphy (*Moral Demands in Nonideal Theory*, New York: Oxford University Press, 2000: pp. 88–93), and Iris Marion Young ('Responsibility and Global Labour Justice', *Journal of Political Philosophy* 12 (2004): 365–388, at 382–383). Tim Mulgan ('Two Conceptions of Benevolence', *Philosophy & Public Affairs* 26 (1997): 62–79) and Miller ('Taking Up the Slack? Responsibility and Justice in Situations of Partial Compliance', in C. Knight & Z. Stemplowska eds. *Responsibility and Distributive Justice*, New York: Oxford University Press, 2011: pp. 230–245, at pp. 238–239) argue that the problem with a duty to do more than one's fair share would be that it would distribute responsibilities incorrectly, but that, plainly, is a roundabout way of appealing to the unfairness of that responsibility being given to the compliers. And, like Ridge ('Fairness and Non-Compliance', in B. Feltham & J. Cottingham eds. *Partiality and Impartiality: Morality, Special Relationships, and the Wider World*, Oxford: Oxford University Press, 2010: p. 194), I think that the same goes for arguments about overdemandingness, which (insofar as they make sense) also amount to arguments about unfairness.

34 There is nevertheless something powerful about the complaint of unfairness or maldistribution. If we think the duties of non-compliers are in effect transferred to compliers, then the former do no wrong, because there's no longer any duty *on them* which they fail to discharge. That – so the complaint goes – infantilises compliers by treating them as less than responsible agents, letting them off the hook. (See L. Murphy *Moral Demands in Nonideal Theory*, New York: Oxford University Press, 2000: p. 113, D. Miller 'Taking Up the Slack? Responsibility and Justice in Situations of Partial Compliance', in C. Knight & Z. Stemplowska eds. *Responsibility and Distributive Justice*, New York: Oxford University Press, 2011: pp. 230–245, at p. 241, and Z. Stemplowska 'Doing More Than One's Fair Share', *Critical Review of International Social and Political Philosophy* 19 (2016): 601 for helpful discussion of this line of thought.) Recognising this as a situation of moral blackmail puts the non-complier back on the hook, even at the same time as acknowledging that the complier has a duty to take up their slack. The non-complier has done the complier wrong, and has a duty to rectify that wrong, and the most straightforward way to do it is to reclaim and discharge the original duty to do their fair share, thereby relieving the complier of the (genuine but unfairly acquired) duty to do it in their stead. My thanks to an anonymous referee for pressing this point.

35 This is another way to read e.g. Miller ('Taking Up the Slack? Responsibility and Justice in Situations of Partial Compliance', in C. Knight & Z. Stemplowska eds. *Responsibility and Distributive Justice*, New York: Oxford University Press, 2011: pp. 230–245). My thanks to Matthew Kramer, Finn McCardel and Adam Rieger for pressing this point.

36 Someone might try to respond to this point by abandoning the intuitively plausible claim that compliers are in fact wronged, and by retreating to the conditional claim that they if there is a duty to take up the slack, then they are wronged. The problem here, of course, is that this generates a *modus tollens* argument against the duty to take up the slack only if there is a non-question-begging reason to think that compliers aren't wronged in this way. My thanks to Matthew Kramer for pressing me on this point.

Conclusion

In this book, I have argued that there exists a phenomenon of moral blackmail. In Chapters 1 and 2, I argued that this should be understood as a species of induced non-voluntary action analogous to coercion: just as the coerced agent acts as they do because the coercer makes the alternatives prudentially unacceptable for them, the morally blackmailed agent acts as they do because the blackmailer makes the alternatives morally unacceptable.

Moral blackmail is bad for various reasons, especially because it affects the victim's responsibility in multiple different ways that become distinguishable if we adopt the pluralistic theory of responsibility that I advocated in Chapters 3 and 4. That theory involves distinguishing between two core concepts of responsibility, explanatory and evaluative, and recognising that the latter especially admits of plural conceptions on which different normative upshots are grounded by different relations between agents and states of affairs. One characteristic of moral blackmail is that it fractures responsibility of different kinds which usually stand together.

The phenomenon of moral blackmail is not just a casuistical curiosity. In Chapters 5 and 6, I showed that it is present in some of the most troubling problems of intergenerational and global justice. Putting it to work in those contexts helps solve those problems, in particular by reconciling their two central but apparently contradictory features: in situations of partial compliance, a dutiful agent can have a real complaint against those (either their ancestors or their delinquent contemporaries) who haven't lived up to their duties, but the dutiful agent is nevertheless under heavier duties as a result of that failure. The resolution offered by moral blackmail is to say that the complaint consists precisely in the imposition of those heavier duties.

So, we end up with a satisfying way forward in those debates about global justice. And we also conclude with further support for the central claim of this book. That my theory of moral blackmail offers that way forward lends inductive support to the idea that it is a useful tool of philosophical analysis. It can, I hope, be deployed with similar utility in other contexts too.

DOI: 10.4324/9781003259619-8

Bibliography

E. Ashford 'The Demandingness of Scanlon's Contractualism', *Ethics* 113 (2003): 273–302.

M. Arvan *Neurofunctional Prudence and Morality: A Philosophical Theory*. New York: Routledge, 2020: pp. 60–89.

B. Barry 'Humanity and Justice in Global Perspective' in J.R. Pennick ed. *NOMOS 24: Ethics, Economics, and the Law*. New York: New York University Press, 1982: pp. 219–252.

S. Bazargan 'Moral Coercion', *Philosophers' Imprint* 14 (2014): 3–5.

T. Beauchamp & J.F. Childress *Principles of Biomedical Ethics* (5th edition). New York: Oxford University Press, 2001.

W. Beckerman 'Intergenerational Equity and the Environment', *Journal of Political Philosophy* 5 (1997): 395–405.

J. Bentham *An Introduction to the Principles of Morals and Legislation*. Originally published 1789. Ed. J.H. Burns & H.L.A. Hart. London: Athlone Press, 1970.

M. Berman 'Blackmail' in J. Deigh & D. Dolinko eds. *The Oxford Handbook of Criminal Law*. Oxford: Oxford University Press, 2011: pp. 37–105.

C. Bertram 'Exploitation and International Justice', *Imprints* 10 (2007): 69–92.

D.O. Brink 'The Nature and Significance of Culpability', *Criminal Law and Philosophy* 13 (2019): 347–373.

D. Brock 'Defending Moral Options', *Philosophy & Phenomenological Research* 51 (1991): 909–931.

A. Buchanan 'Justice and Charity', *Ethics* 97 (1987): 558–575.

C. Carr 'Coercion and Freedom', *American Philosophical Quarterly* 25 (1988): 59–67.

I. Carter *A Measure of Freedom*. New York: Oxford University Press, 1999.

A. Chakravartty *A Metaphysics for Scientific Realism*. Cambridge: Cambridge University Press, 2007.

L.J. Cohen 'Who Is Starving Whom?', *Theoria* 2 (1981): 76.

B. Colburn 'The Concept of Voluntariness', *Journal of Political Philosophy* 16 (2008): 101–111.

B. Colburn *Autonomy and Liberalism*. New York: Routledge, 2010.

B. Colburn 'In Defence of Comprehensive Liberalism', *Philosophy and Public Issues* 2 (2012): 17–29.

B. Colburn 'Autonomy and End of Life Decisions – A Paradox' in J. Räikkä and J. Varelius eds. *Adaptation and Autonomy: Sour Grapes in Life and Death Choices*. New York: Springer, 2013: pp. 69–80.

B. Colburn 'Dramatic Vignettes in Moral Inquiry', *Social Analysis* 68 (2024): 66–74.

E.J. Craig 'The Practical Explication of Knowledge', *Proceedings of the Aristotelian Society* 87 (1986–1987): 211–226.

E.J. Craig *Knowledge and the State of Nature*. Oxford: Clarendon Press, 1990.

G. Dworkin *The Theory and Practice of Autonomy*. Cambridge: Cambridge University Press, 1988.

R. Dworkin Sovereign Virtue. Cambridge, MA: Harvard University Press, 2000.

J. Feinberg *Harm to Self*. New York: Oxford University Press, 1986.

H. Frankfurt 'Alternative Possibilities and Moral Responsibility', *Journal of Philosophy* 66 (1969): 829–839.

H. Frankfurt 'Freedom of the Will and the Concept of a Person', *Journal of Philosophy* 68 (1971): 5–20.

H. Frankfurt *The Importance of What We Care About*. Cambridge: Cambridge University Press, 1988.

M. Fricker 'The Relativism of Blame and William's Relativism of Distance', *Proceedings of the Aristotelian Society Supplementary Volume* 84 (2010): 151–177.

M. Fricker 'What's the Point of Blame? A Paradigm Based Explanation', *Noûs* 50 (2016): 165–183.

S.M. Gardiner 'Accepting Collective Responsibility for the Future', *Journal of Practical Ethics* 5 (2017): 22–52.

S.M. Gardiner 'The Threat of Intergenerational Extortion: On the Temptation to Become the Climate Mafia, Masquerading as an Intergenerational Robin Hood', *Canadian Journal of Philosophy* 47 (2017): 368–394.

M. Garnett 'Ignorance, Incompetence, and the Concept of Liberty', *Journal of Political Philosophy* 15 (2007): 428–446.

M. Garnett 'Coercion: The Wrong and the Bad', *Ethics* 128 (2018): 545–573.

B. Gert 'Coercion and Freedom' in J.R. Pennock & J.W. Chapman eds. *Coercion*. Piscataway, NJ: Transaction Publishers, 1972: pp. 30–48.

C. Hempel *Aspects of Scientific Explanation and Other Essays in the Philosophy of Science*. New York: Free Press, 1965.

W. Hohfeld *Fundamental Legal Conceptions as Applied in Judicial Reasoning*. New Haven, CT: Yale University Press, 1917.

B. Hooker 'Rule-Consequentialism, Incoherence, Fairness', *Proceedings of the Aristotelian Society* 95 (1994): 19–35.

S. Hurley Justice, *Luck and Knowledge*. Cambridge, MA: Harvard University Press, 2003.

IPCC Climate Change 2022: Impacts, *Adaptation, and Vulnerability*. Contribution of Working Group II to the Sixth Assessment Report of the Intergovernmental Panel on Climate Change. Eds. H.-O. Pörtner et al., Cambridge: Cambridge University Press, 2022.

S. Kagan *The Limits of Morality*. Oxford: Clarendon Press 1989.

I. Kant *Grundlegung zur Metaphysik der Sitten*. Originally published 1785. Ed. & trans. M. Gregor as *Groundwork of the Metaphysics of Morals*. Cambridge: Cambridge University Press, 1994.

S. Keller 'Fiduciary Duties and Moral Blackmail', *The Journal of Applied Philosophy* 35 (2018): 481–495.

C. Knight Luck Egalitarianism: *Equality, Responsibility, and Justice*. Edinburgh: Edinburgh University Press, 2009.

M.H. Kramer, N.E. Simmonds & H. Steiner *A Debate over Rights.* Oxford: Oxford University Press, 2000.

M.H. Kramer *The Quality of Freedom.* Oxford: Oxford University Press, 2003.

M. Lane 'States of Nature, Epistemic and Political', *Proceedings of the Aristotelian Society* 99 (1999): 211–224.

M. Lange Because without Cause*: Non-Causal Explanations in Science and Mathematics*. Oxford: Oxford University Press, 2017.

P. Lipton 'Causation and Explanation' in H. Beebee, C. Hitchcock & P. Menzies eds. *The Oxford Handbook of Causation.* Oxford: Oxford University Press, 1999: pp. 619–631.

P. Lipton *Inference to the Best Explanation* (2nd edition). London: Routledge, 2004.

S. Loriaux 'Beneficence and Distributive Justice in a Globalising World', *Global Society* 20 (2006): 251–265.

J.R. Lucas *The Principles of Politics.* Oxford: Clarendon Press, 1966.

G. MacCallum 'Negative and Positive Freedom', *Philosophical Review* 76 (1967): 312–334.

C. Mackenzie & N. Stoljar eds. *Relational Autonomy: Feminist Perspectives on Autonomy, Agency, and the Social Self.* New York: Oxford University Press, 2000.

C. Mantzavinos *Explanatory Pluralism*. Cambridge: Cambridge University Press, 2016.

A. Mason *Levelling the Playing Field.* New York: Oxford University Press, 2006.

E. Mason 'Coercion and Integrity' in M. Timmons ed. *Oxford Studies in Normative Ethics* Vol. 2. New York: Oxford University Press, 2012: pp. 180–205.

T. McConnell 'Moral Blackmail', *Ethics* 91 (1981): 544–567.

E. McTernan 'How to Be a Responsibility-Sensitive Egalitarian: From Metaphysics to Social Practice', *Political Studies* 64 (2016): 748–764.

L.H. Meyer & D. Rose 'Enough for the Future' in A. Gosseries & L.H. Meyer eds. *Intergenerational Justice*. Oxford: Oxford University Press, 2009: pp. 219–248.

J.S. Mill, *On Liberty*. Originally published 1859. In S. Collini ed. On Liberty *and* Other Writings. Cambridge: Cambridge University Press, 1989: pp. 1–116.

J.S. Mill Utilitarianism. Ed. G. Sher. Indianapolis, IN: Hackett, 2001.

D. Miller 'Taking Up the Slack? Responsibility and Justice in Situations of Partial Compliance' in C. Knight & Z. Stemplowska eds. Responsibility and Distributive Justice. New York: Oxford University Press, 2011: pp. 230–245.

M.S. Moore 'The Strictness of Strict Liability', *Criminal Law and Philosophy* 12 (2018): 513–529.

T. Mulgan 'Two Conceptions of Benevolence', *Philosophy & Public Affairs* 26 (1997): 62–79.

L. Murphy *Moral Demands in Nonideal Theory.* New York: Oxford University Press, 2000.

R.H. Myers 'The Inescapability of Moral Reasons', *Philosophy and Phenomenological Research* 59 (1999): 281–307.

J. Narveson 'Welfare and Wealth: Poverty and Justice in Today's World', *The Journal of Ethics* 8 (2004): 305–348.

R. Nozick 'Coercion' in P. Lazlett & W. Runciman eds. *Philosophy, Politics, and Society* (4th series). Oxford: Blackwell, 1967: pp. 101–135.

R. Nozick Anarchy, *State, and Utopia.* New York: Basic Books, 1974.

S. Olsaretti 'Freedom, Force and Choice: Against the Rights-Based Definition of Voluntariness', *Journal of Political Philosophy* 6 (1998): 53–78.

S. Olsaretti 'The Value of Freedom and Freedom of Choice', *Politeia* 56 (2000): 114–121.

S. Olsaretti Liberty, *Desert and the Market.* Cambridge: Cambridge University Press, 2004.

S. Olsaretti 'The Concept of Voluntariness – A Reply', *Journal of Political Philosophy* 16 (2008): 112–121.

S. Olsaretti 'Responsibility and the Consequences of Choice', *Proceedings of the Aristotelian Society* 109 (2009): pp. 165–188.

M. Oshana 'Ascriptions of Responsibility', *American Philosophical Quarterly* 34 (1997): 71–83.

M. Oshana *Personal Autonomy in Society*. Aldershot: Ashgate, 2006.

D. Owen 'Refugees, Fairness and Taking up the Slack', *Moral Philosophy and Politics* 3 (2016): 141–164.

D. Parfit *Reasons and Persons*. Oxford: Oxford University Press, 1984.

C. Pincock 'Accommodating Explanatory Pluralism' in A. Reutlinger & J. Saatsi eds. *Explanation Beyond Causation: Philosophical Perspectives on Non-Causal Explanations*. Oxford: Oxford University Press, 2018: pp. 39–56.

Plato 'Gorgias' in M. Schofield ed. & T. Griffin trans. Plato: Gorgias, Menexenus, Protagoras. Cambridge: Cambridge University Press, 2009: pp. 1–114.

S. Psillos *Scientific Realism: How Science Tracks Truth*. London: Routledge, 1999.

S. Psillos *Causation and Explanation*, Cheshunt: Acumen, 2002.

A. Rajczi 'The Argument from Self-Creation: A Refutation of Act-Consequentialism and a Defence of Moral Options', *American Philosophical Quarterly* 48 (2011): 315–332.

J. Rawls *Political Liberalism*. New York: Columbia University Press, 1993.

J. Raz *The Morality of Freedom*. Oxford: Clarendon Press, 1986.

M. Rendall 'Non-Identity, Sufficiency and Exploitation', *Journal of Political Philosophy* 19 (2011): 229–247.

M. Ridge 'Fairness and Non-Compliance' in B. Feltham & J. Cottingham eds. *Partiality and Impartiality: Morality, Special Relationships, and the Wider World.* Oxford: Oxford University Press, 2010: pp. 194–222.

M.A. Roberts, *'The Nonidentity Problem'* in E.N. Zalta & U. *Nodeman eds. The Stanford Encyclopedia of Philosophy. https://plato.stanford.edu/archives/win2022/entries/nonidentity-problem/* [accessed 11 March 2024].

J.E. Roemer *Equality of Opportunity.* Cambridge MA: Harvard University Press, 1998.

C.C. Ryan 'The Normative Concept of Coercion', *Mind* 89 (1090): 481–498.

W. Salmon *Four Decades of Scientific Explanation.* Minneapolis: University of Minnesota Press, 1989.

W. Salmon 'Why Ask 'Why'?' in his *Causality and Explanation*. Oxford: Oxford University Press, 1998.

T.M. Scanlon 'The Significance of Choice' in S. McMullin ed. *The Tanner Lectures on Human Values*, Vol. 8. Salt Lake City: University of Utah Press, 1988a: pp. 149–216.

T.M. Scanlon *What We Owe to Each Other.* Cambridge MA: Harvard University Press, 1998b.

A. Simester ed. *Appraising Strict Liability*. Oxford: Oxford University Press 2005.

P. Singer 'Family, Affluence, and Morality', *Philosophy & Public Affairs* 1 (1972): 229–243.

M. Smith *The Moral Problem*. Oxford: Blackwell, 1994.

D. Smolkin 'Toward a Rights-Based Solution to the Non-Identity Problem', *Journal of Social Philosophy* 30 (1999): 193–208.

H. Steiner 'Individual Liberty', *Proceedings of the Aristotelian Society* 75 (1974): 33–50.

H. Steiner *An Essay on Rights.* Oxford: Blackwell, 1994.

H. Steiner 'Are There Still Any Natural Rights?' in M.H. Kramer, C. Grant, B. Colburn & A. Hatzistavrou eds. *The Legacy of H.L.A. Hart.* Oxford: Oxford University Press, 2008: pp. 239–250.

Z. Stemplowska 'Holding People Responsible for What They Do Not Control', *Philosophy, Politics & Economics* 7 (2008): 355–377.

Z. Stemplowksa 'Making Justice Sensitive to Responsibility', *Political Studies* 57 (2009): 237–259.

Z. Stemplowksa 'Doing More Than One's Fair Share', *Critical Review of International Social and Political Philosophy* 19 (2016): 591–608.

P. Unger *Living High and Letting Die.* New York: Oxford University Press, 1996.

L. Valentini *Justice in a Globalized World: A Normative Framework.* New York: Oxford University Press, 2011.

P. Vallentyne 'Brute Luck and Responsibility', *Politics, Philosophy & Economics* 7 (2008): 57–80.

B. Van Frassen *The Scientific Image.* Oxford: Oxford University Press, 1980.

B. Van Frassen *The Empirical Stance.* New Haven, CT: Yale University Press, 2002.

Wacky Races. Hanna-Barbera Productions, for CBS. WBBM-TV, Chicago, 1968–1969.

G. Watson 'Two Faces of Responsibility', *Philosophical Topics* 24 (1996): 227–248.

L. Wenar 'The Nature of Rights', *Philosophy & Public Affairs* 33 (2005): 223–253.

L. Wenar 'The Analysis of Rights' in M.H. Kramer, C. Grant, B. Colburn & A. Hatzistavrou eds. *The Legacy of H.L.A. Hart.* Oxford: Oxford University Press, 2008: pp. 251–275.

A. Wertheimer *Coercion.* Princeton NJ: Princeton University Press, 1988.

S. White 'On the Moral Objection to Coercion', *Philosophy & Public Affairs* 45 (2017): 199–231.

B. Williams 'Voluntary Acts and Responsible Agents', *Oxford Journal of Legal Studies* 10 (1990): 1–10.

B. Williams *Making Sense of Humanity, and Other Philosophical Papers.* Cambridge: Cambridge University Press, 1995.

B. Williams *Truth and Truthfulness.* Princeton NJ: Princeton University Press, 2002.

S. Wolf 'Asymmetrical Freedom', *Journal of Philosophy* 77 (1980): 151–166.

J. Woodward 'The Non-Identity Problem', *Ethics* 96 (1986): 804–831.

J. Woodward *Making Things Happen: A Theory of Causal Explanation.* Oxford: Oxford University Press, 2003.

G. Yaffe 'Indoctrination, Coercion, and Freedom of Will', *Philosophy and Phenomenological Research* 67 (2003): 335–356.

I.M. Young 'Responsibility and Global Labour Justice', *Journal of Political Philosophy* 12 (2004): 365–388.

D. Zimmerman 'Coercive Wage Offers', *Philosophy & Public Affairs* 20 (1981): 121–125.

Index

Note: Page numbers followed by "n" denote endnotes.

For Product Safety Concerns and Information please contact our EU representative GPSR@taylorandfrancis.com
Taylor & Francis Verlag GmbH, Kaufingerstraße 24, 80331 München, Germany

www.ingramcontent.com/pod-product-compliance
Lightning Source LLC
LaVergne TN
LVHW010941110826
845149LV00013B/2708